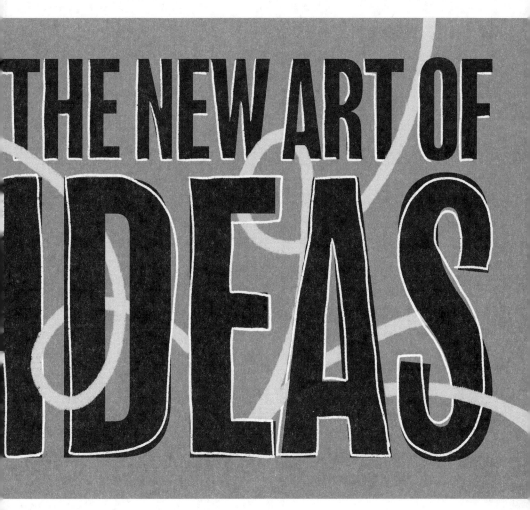

THE NEW ART OF IDEAS

THE NEW ART OF
IDEAS
UNLOCK YOUR CREATIVE POTENTIAL

ROBIN LANDA

ILLUSTRATED BY HOLLY TAYLOR

FOREWORD BY LORIN LATARRO

BK

Berrett–Koehler Publishers, Inc.

Berrett-Koehler Publishers, Inc.
1333 Broadway, Suite 1000
Oakland, CA 94612-1921
Tel: (510) 817-2277 | Fax: (510) 817-2278
www.bkconnection.com

ORDERING INFORMATION

QUANTITY SALES. Special discounts are available on quantity purchases by corporations, associations, and others. For details, contact the "Special Sales Department" at the Berrett-Koehler address above.

INDIVIDUAL SALES. Berrett-Koehler publications are available through most bookstores. They can also be ordered directly from Berrett-Koehler: Tel: (800) 929-2929; Fax: (802) 864-7626; www.bkconnection.com.

ORDERS FOR COLLEGE TEXTBOOK/COURSE ADOPTION USE. Please contact Berrett-Koehler: Tel: (800) 929-2929; Fax: (802) 864-7626.

Distributed to the U.S. trade and internationally by Penguin Random House Publisher Services.

Berrett-Koehler and the BK logo are registered trademarks of Berrett-Koehler Publishers, Inc.

Printed in the United States of America

Berrett-Koehler books are printed on long-lasting acid-free paper. When it is available, we choose paper that has been manufactured by environmentally responsible processes. These may include using trees grown in sustainable forests, incorporating recycled paper, minimizing chlorine in bleaching, or recycling the energy produced at the paper mill.

Library of Congress Cataloging-in-Publication Data
Names: Landa, Robin, author. | Taylor, Holly, illustrator.
Title: The new art of ideas : unlock your creative potential / Robin Landa ; illustrated by Holly Taylor.
Description: First Edition. | Oakland, CA : Berrett-Koehler Publishers, [2023] | Includes bibliographical references and index.
Identifiers: LCCN 2022017357 (print) | LCCN 2022017358 (ebook) | ISBN 9781523002078 (paperback) | ISBN 9781523002085 (pdf) | ISBN 9781523002092 (epub) | ISBN 9781523002108 (audiobook)
Subjects: LCSH: Creative ability in business. | Goal (Psychology)
Classification: LCC HD53 .L3625 2023 (print) | LCC HD53 (ebook) | DDC 650.1—dc23/eng/20220729
LC record available at https://lccn.loc.gov/2022017357
LC ebook record available at https://lccn.loc.gov/2022017358

First Edition

30 29 28 27 26 25 24 23 22 ‖ 10 9 8 7 6 5 4 3 2 1

Book production: BookMatters
Front cover design and interior illustrations: © 2023 by Holly Taylor

To Harry, my forever tango partner

CONTENTS

FOREWORD

I am no stranger to developing an idea from nothing. As a choreographer for Broadway, operas, and films, I begin with an empty room and create and layer dance upon dance. The beauty of Robin Landa's book? *The New Art of Ideas* reveals fundamental truths about creation of any sort. Her method works for anyone interested in creating for the betterment of the world.

To have a vision is a uniquely human experience. Many of us have a vision, a eureka moment, an idea—Robin Landa gives the reader a focused way forward to help push the vision toward its finished idea. A *goal* is a noble pursuit, but it is easy to lose sight of the idea along the way, to give up, to fizzle out. This instructive book provides key navigation tools to get the reader to the finish line.

I especially love the pieces in this creation puzzle about observation and the *gap*. Looking at the world with curiosity is fundamental to creation. Looking and listening closely are hallmarks of success. Landa cites countless examples of how a small, focused observation changed the world.

And then, the *why* of it all. Why is this idea a worthwhile pursuit? What does the world *gain* from this idea? What is the idea's additive value? All worthy questions for the creator to ponder. As an artist,

I always ask why—and I am always searching for a story to tell that brings something special to an audience: to learn, to receive, to question, to observe. Robin Landa's method works for ideas, for inventions, for dances, for plays, and more.

I am sure you, the reader, will finish the book with more confidence, clarity, and excitement about whatever you are dreaming up.

What do *you* wish existed in the world?

Lorin Latarro

Lorin Latarro choreographed Broadway's *Mrs. Doubtfire, Into the Woods, Les Liaisons Dangereuses,* The Public Theater's *The Visitor,* Broadway-bound *The Outsiders,* and *Like Water for Chocolate.* She choreographed Broadway and London productions of *Waitress* as well as *La Traviata* at the Metropolitan Opera. Latarro is directing Candace Bushnell's one-woman show *Is There Still Sex in the City?*

INTRODUCTION

UNLOCK YOUR CREATIVE POTENTIAL

Our industry does not respect tradition.
What it respects is innovation.
SATYA NADELLA, CEO, MICROSOFT

It was a scroll through Twitter that started it—the photo of a custom gaming controller adapted for an injured vet. When Matt Hite saw the photo, his keen eye and curiosity urged him to find out more. Hite has that kind of mind, and it was thrown into action by an observant moment on Twitter. Serendipitous, yes. But what Hite did next ignited a goal that would change many lives.

When Hite, a Microsoft engineer, saw that photo, he reached out to Ken Jones, a mechanical engineer and avid gamer who had founded Warfighter Engaged, a nonprofit organization that provides bespoke adapted gaming controllers to wounded veterans. Warfighter's one engineer designs each gaming controller to meet the needs of a single vet, making it challenging to fulfill the hundreds of requests the organization receives every month.

Jones's mission is to improve the lives of warfighters living with disabilities—triple amputees, quadriplegics, veterans with traumatic brain injuries, veterans with prosthetics, and other wounded veterans. During his conversation with Jones, Hite learned about the overwhelming challenges injured veterans face when trying to access the world of gaming. These vets, Jones explained, were being left out of the fun and therapeutic experiences gaming has to offer. There was a gap in the gaming hardware industry for 46 million gamers living with disabilities in the United States alone.[1]

For many people, gaming isn't just a hobby—it's a passion and a way of connecting. If you're a gamer, or you know a gamer, you understand what I mean. For people with limited mobility—whether by birth or because of an accident or war injury—the gaming experience is different. For many, the standard configuration—the positioning of the jacks across the back of the device, the shape and edges, and the position of the controls and buttons, among other design issues—makes it difficult to navigate. When Jones saw a gap, he set a goal. Through his organization and humanitarian efforts, he helped deliver gains to wounded veterans. After speaking with Jones, Hite decided that he too was going to do something about that gap.

Every year Microsoft holds an Ability Summit that brings together people who have disabilities, designers, engineers, and marketers. The idea is to identify where Microsoft can speed up innovation to improve accessibility for people living with disabilities—both in the company and outside of the company—on the pathway to a more inclusive society.[2] Hite put together a hackathon project team at the Ability Summit to tackle the design problem facing Warfighter Engaged. On his LinkedIn bio, Matt Hite writes,

> In early 2015, I founded a Microsoft hackathon project at our internal Ability summit. The central piece was what I first dubbed "an Accessibility Breakout box" with the goal of injecting external switch input directly into a regular Xbox controller....
>
> That project blossomed into something I never imagined possible....It became what is now known as the Xbox Adaptive Controller. After years of hard work at Microsoft, my dream finally became a reality. I can't begin to express how much that means to

me.... Because EVERYONE should be able to experience the joy of gaming.[3]

At that initial hackathon, the team worked with Jones to develop a gaming device. The project won the hackathon's top prize. During subsequent Microsoft hackathons, other teams further refined the device.

This work coincided with other efforts at Microsoft to improve accessibility. In 2015, Kris Hunter, the director of devices user research and hardware accessibility for Microsoft Experiences and Devices, and Bryce Johnson, a senior Xbox designer, had launched the Gaming for Everyone initiative, housed in Microsoft's Inclusive Tech Lab.[4]

As Microsoft's leadership recognized the value of this project, interest grew within the company. Microsoft's project team partnered with experts, turning to gamers, accessibility advocates, and nonprofits that worked with gamers who have disabilities, such as the AbleGamers Charity, the Cerebral Palsy Foundation, SpecialEffect, Warfighter Engaged, and community members. According to the Xbox website, "Input from these groups has helped shape the design, functionality, and packaging of the Xbox Adaptive Controller."[5]

An adaptive controller that makes gaming more inclusive is a worthwhile idea. Many gamers have limited mobility, may be missing a limb or hand, or do not have the strength or coordination necessary to use a conventional controller. Yet the development of the Xbox Adaptive Controller took several years and relied on many ardent believers. The Microsoft Xbox project manager had to make a strong case to Microsoft to bring it to market. "Trying to develop a business case for an accessible product can be very, very challenging, because the scale of the products don't generally make a positive business case for the investment that has to go in," said Leo Castillo, who served as the general manager for Xbox hardware when the controller was under development.[6]

This is a case where the return on corporate investment is not simply financial—it is a gain for a community of people. The Xbox Adaptive Controller is the first one designed and manufactured at a large scale by a leading technology company.

To tell their success story, Microsoft and its advertising agency, McCann New York, gathered a group of young gamers living with disabilities, kids with limited mobility and some who are missing hands, and gave them starring roles in a Super Bowl commercial. McCann's advertising idea swept up industry awards and people's hearts.

"My name is Ian."

"My name is Taylor."

"My name is Owen, and I am nine-and-a-half years old. I want to show you the Xbox Adaptive Controller." Owen went on to demonstrate how to set up the one-handed joystick with the Xbox Adaptive Controller.

The young cast taught everyone how to open the package (accessible from the start), set up, and use the new controller. "I can hit the buttons just as fast as they can," said Taylor while demonstrating.

Owen's dad said, "One of the biggest fears early on was: How will Owen be viewed by the other kids? He's not different when he plays."[7] With this accessible tech, Owen can enjoy gaming alongside everyone else.

Further, injured veterans and millions of others in the accessibility community can also gain by using the Adaptive Controller and can be included in any game. *Time* magazine considered the Xbox Adaptive Controller among the best inventions of 2018.

This book is about precisely that—how to get great ideas. Not just lots of ideas, but ideas worth pursuing.

There are, of course, other approaches to generating ideas, like brainstorming. *The New Art of Ideas* doesn't replace brainstorming. If brainstorming works for you, by all means keep using it. Or use question-storming: instead of generating as many solutions as possible, as in brainstorming, you generate as many questions as possible, which might point you in a better direction.

You can follow a conventional process of combining two existing ideas into a single new idea. That certainly works, but it's only one way to generate an idea. If that's the only method you use, you're limiting your thinking and not necessarily generating *worthwhile* ideas.

Another go-to method is a five-stage process: (1) preparation: conduct research and brainstorm to spark an idea; (2) incubation: allow the information and thoughts you've generated to incubate; (3) illumination: in an "aha" moment, bring everything together into an idea; (4) evaluation: check the validity of your idea; and (5) verification: bring the idea to life. But this process doesn't explain how everything comes together in that "aha" moment or how to evaluate the validity of the idea. That is where *The New Art of Ideas* comes in.

Unlike the conventional books about brainstorming or generating as many ideas as possible no matter how good they are, this book focuses on generating good ideas that have value, ideas that can make a difference to individuals' lives, to society, and to our planet. You'll learn how to separate the wheat from the chaff.

The value of *The New Art of Ideas* is this: When you identify a *goal*, a *gap*, and a *gain*, then you know your consequent idea will have value.

A goal alone is not enough. Having a goal doesn't make it worthwhile—it might be a ridiculous goal or a goal that will cause harm to individuals, society, business, creatures, or the environment. Recently, we've seen too many examples of people who "lure investors to bankroll ideas that turn out to be stupid, evil, or fraudulent."[8] When you determine that your *goal* fills a *gap* and produces a *gain*, you'll know it's not ridiculous, will not cause harm, and will be needed or wanted.

No other framework points you in this direction—that is, on the path to ideas worth pursuing.

The Three Gs is a new way of thinking, a new framework for ideation. Anyone can use it effectively. As a consultant and professor, I have witnessed people from diverse backgrounds, disciplines, and careers—everyone from engineers in their innovation labs to brand managers at major corporations to creative professionals who must generate dozens of ideas daily—start to approach idea generation differently, with better outcomes and far less frustration. In fact, thousands of creative professionals whose careers demand the generation of many ideas on a daily basis can do so because they studied with me.

The New Art of Ideas

When you read about a worthwhile idea, such as Microsoft's Xbox Adaptive Controller, it's useful to deconstruct the underlying thinking.

The model framework I'm proposing is brand new. After examining lots of great ideas and teaching people how to generate ideas for many years, I formulated this framework. In each of the examples I discuss in the book, you can identify a goal, a gap, and a gain.

Goal + Gap + Gain → Worthwhile Idea

The Microsoft engineer had a *goal*—to create accessible gaming technology for people living with disabilities. He and his colleagues at Microsoft filled a *gap* in product design. It was a huge *gain* for gamers living with disabilities, who benefited greatly from the idea and design of an accessible device.

The Three Gs—goal, gap, and gain—unlock an idea. The Three Gs can help you understand what a worthwhile idea is, how it works, and how to generate one. Furthermore, the Three Gs yield ideas that move the needle, ideas that are not inconsequential but worthwhile, ideas that will make a difference because you are seeking an outcome with a benefit for individuals, society, or our planet.

Audiences and Uses

This book is a step-by-step guide to generating, crystallizing, or amplifying worthwhile ideas. Although appropriate for almost anyone, it will be especially helpful to five types of audiences:

1. Individuals in a professional, technical, creative, or support role who want to make a difference in what they do and in the world will find this book valuable in helping them generate worthwhile ideas based on their own aspirations or to make progress in an organization.

2. Independent consultants, whether external or internal, will find this book valuable for their growth and success because we are living in an idea economy. This audience includes consultants, coaches, contractors, counselors, mentors, and advisors who need to demonstrate their ability to innovate, think creatively, and contribute to the growth and progress of a business, organization, or community. This book provides the keys to unlocking worthwhile ideas and creative potential.

3. Experienced professionals will find this book helpful to over-come a temporary creative block or kick-start a stalled career. Some professionals, even those with a wealth of experience, may be stuck in a position where they feel stagnant or are not learning. This book will show you how to broaden your thinking to demonstrate the value you can contribute to any company or organization's growth, progress, or innovation. The Three Gs ideation skill will attract the attention of others, and you will gain the recognition and success you need.

4. Leaders, team leaders, managers, and project managers will find this book a valuable resource for guiding their teams and enhancing the team's performance across the board. In most cases, a team's work reflects the team leader's perfor-mance. The Three Gs framework is a practical way for small, medium-size, and large organizations to use strategic creative thinking to get ahead of the competition in an idea-based economy. You can also use the chapter on diversity, equity, and inclusion (DEI) to amplify the Three Gs system.

5. Faculty in almost every field are trying to get their students to generate worthwhile ideas. The Three Gs are easy for college and university students to remember and implement—I know because I use them effectively in my classroom. I've taught thousands of university students who have gone on to rewarding creative careers. Alumni tell me that this process helps them stay ahead of their peers on the job. This book thus might supplement or replace the method you're now using.

Welcome to *The New Art of Ideas*—the Three Gs will unlock your creative potential. Because everyone is worthy of learning to gen-erate a worthwhile idea!

NOTES: YOUR IDEAS

Make a wish list for making the world just a bit, or a whole lot, better. You're just musing right now.

CHAPTER 1

THE NEW ART OF IDEAS

Discovery consists of seeing what everybody has
seen and thinking what nobody has thought.
ALBERT SZENT-GYÖRGYI

One semester, I had a student who was academically underprepared and required so much attention that his needs were hampering my ability to teach the other students in the class. To support this student and allow myself the class time to work with everyone equally, I thought: *How can I make him more independent during class time?* I remembered Dale, my former dance instructor, who had told me he used a checklist before every performance. "Pilots use checklists with step-by-step checks for takeoff, flight, landing, and taxiing," he said, "so why not dancers?"

What if I devised a design checklist for this student, similar to a pilot's checklist?

My *goal* was to help this student be more independent and prepared. This design checklist filled a *gap* in my instructional methods. The checklist covered all of the major design principles—balance, flow, unity, visual hierarchy, emphasis, rhythm, and so on—along with their definitions. The student could use the checklist to critique his own work, ticking off each box—each principle—to ensure that his composition worked to communicate his idea.

In fact, all of the students—the high achievers, this underprepared fellow, and everyone in between—would *gain* from using a checklist to critique their own thinking and design solutions. Since then, I have devised and published several checklists for different aspects of design and advertising, and they are used by instructors, professionals, and students worldwide. Not a big idea per se, but one that has served its purpose a thousand-fold.

To get to a worthwhile idea—big or small—use *The New Art of Ideas* framework's Three Gs: goal, gap, and gain. Here's how it works.

A *goal* is your aim, what you want to achieve. Let's say your goal is to design a shape-shifting concept car. Direct your efforts at researching and developing that car concept. Your goal compels you to focus your thinking, energy, and resources.

Determine if the goal will fill a *gap*. Is there a missing piece in research, the arts, business, or product development? Is there an area that has been underexplored or not explored at all? The gap could be any number of things: a type, a size, a location, an analysis, a system, a product, choreography, music, art, arts fusion, marketing, design, song cycle genres, and more.

Finally, is there a benefit in there for someone, for society, or for our planet? What do they *gain* from your goal and from filling this gap? This gain can apply to a community, a company, an entire industry, and so on. If there's no benefit, there's no point in filling a gap—or perhaps there was no gap to begin with.

The gap and the gain aren't as direct or clearly defined in innovations or creations in the arts as they are when someone invents a medical device or a sustainable farming system. Nonetheless, the arts are critical to people's well-being and inspire thinking and creativity. All great art is transformative because it allows us to understand ourselves more deeply, as a part of the greater world. All one needs to do is think of an installation by Yayoi Kusama, choreography by Luis Salgado, a poem by Amanda Gorman, songs by Fiona Apple, or a film by Lulu Wang to realize how the arts nourish us, inspire us, transport us, and connect us to each other, to creatures, and to our planet.

SPOTLIGHT *HAMILTON* BY LIN-MANUEL MIRANDA

During the late summer of 2007, Lin-Manuel Miranda, an award-winning composer, lyricist, and actor, wanted something to read while vacationing in Mexico. He picked up Ron Chernow's biography *Alexander Hamilton,* which was a best seller and had been named a finalist for the National Book Critics Circle Award. Most people wouldn't think of a historical biography as a beach read, but Miranda credits his father, political advisor Luis A. Miranda, for his interest in history and politics.

Immediately attracted to the Hamilton biography, Miranda selected the book thinking the story of the Hamilton/Burr duel would inspire a "jokey-rap thing." As Miranda was reading the biography, he realized, "Hamilton's whole life was about the power of words and wouldn't it be great to hear a hip-hop album about how we created this country?" he told Robert Viagas of *Playbill.*[1]

What Miranda's choice reveals is his wide-ranging intellectual curiosity, his desire to feed his thinking even while on vacation, and his understanding of environmental context—that the factor of rest, which typically comes with a vacation, allows one's thoughts to percolate.

"It's no accident that the best idea I've ever had in my life—perhaps maybe the best one I'll ever have in my life—came to me on vacation," Miranda told *Huffington Post* editor-in-chief Arianna Huffington in a livestream interview. "When I picked up Ron Chernow's biography [of Hamilton], I was at a resort in Mexico on my first vacation from *In the Heights,* which I had been working seven years to bring to Broadway," he continued. "The moment my brain got a moment's rest, *Hamilton* walked into it."[2]

Before Chernow's Hamilton biography and Miranda's hit musical, many people thought of Hamilton (1755–1804)—George Washington's aide-de-camp in the Continental Army, coauthor of the Federalist Papers, founder of the Bank of New York, and the first treasury secretary of the United States—as the fellow who died in a legendary duel with Aaron Burr in July 1804. Hamilton, a largely self-taught orphan from the Caribbean, appeared on the American political scene seemingly out of nowhere. He greatly influenced George Washington and profoundly helped shape the young nation. Most people, however, misunderstood Hamilton's critical role in building the foundations of the United States. In *Alexander Hamilton*, Chernow writes, "Today, we are indisputably the heirs to Hamilton's America, and to repudiate his legacy is, in many ways, to repudiate the modern world."[3]

You could say the path to Miranda's megahit starts with the fascinating life of the first treasury secretary of the United States, or at least with Chernow, who set out to give Hamilton, a relentless champion of ideas, his due.

Miranda's first musical, *In the Heights,* opened on Broadway and went on to win the 2008 Tony Award for Best Musical. During its theatrical Broadway run, Miranda conceived his *Hamilton* project as a hip-hop concept mixtape. In an interview with *Playbill,* Miranda said he viewed Hamilton as brilliant yet self-destructive for getting into fights with Thomas Jefferson, John Adams, and Aaron Burr, the last one resulting in his death. Miranda said, while reading the biography,

> I'm thinking "This is Biggie, this is Tupac...this is hip-hop!" As
> I'm writing, I'm imagining these dream rappers playing specific
> roles. There's a point in one song where I'm just doing a bad

Busta Rhymes impression on the demo because I just can't picture anyone but Busta Rhymes doing it. In my ideal vision for this project, we get really amazing rappers to play these different parts.[4]

Miranda was already conceiving the Founding Fathers as hip-hop artists!

As part of the 2009 White House Evening of Poetry, Music, and the Spoken Word, President Barack Obama invited Miranda to perform. The Obamas and the other fortunate members of the White House audience heard the public debut of the opening song from Miranda's project, then titled "The Hamilton Mixtape." Heartened by the White House audience's enthusiastic reaction to his work, Miranda went on to write another song for "The Hamilton Mixtape," "My Shot." A year later, Miranda called his project a "hip-hop song cycle." In 2012, on what would have been Hamilton's 255th birthday, he presented it as part of the 14th season of Lincoln Center's American Songbook series. By the summer of 2013, Miranda's hip-hop song cycle, "The Hamilton Mixtape," was taking shape as a stage musical.

Miranda changed the language of Broadway musicals. He is a MacArthur Fellow, and his greatest work to date, *Hamilton*, won the 2016 Pulitzer Prize for drama.

Let's look at Miranda's thinking through the lens of the Three Gs. Miranda set a *goal*—to write a hip-hop song cycle, "The Hamilton Mixtape," about Alexander Hamilton and then expanded his goal. He recognized the creative potential of his idea. The *gap* in musical theater? No other musical had ever employed hip-hop as the dominant musical genre (the music of Miranda's *In the Heights* embraces several musical genres, including hip-hop) and cross-casting to tell the story of America's Founding Fathers. The *gain?* Miranda expanded the musical theater genre and informed, inspired, and entertained millions.

By anyone's standards, Miranda is creative. I know what you're thinking: he won a MacArthur genius grant; he's in an elite category of thinkers. You're correct. However, by analyzing his work through the Three Gs, you and I can start to see how he might have formed his idea. Analyzing the works of others provides insights that will help you unlock your own creative potential.

◉ SPOTLIGHT   LOOOP / H&M

If you've ever cleaned out your closet only to load up a huge bag or two of clothing to throw out or donate, imagine all the fast fashion that ends up that way. Did you know that 85% of clothing ends up in a landfill or incinerator?[5] Even much donated clothing is dumped. This unwanted fashion often ends its journey by causing an environmental catastrophe: it might take hundreds or thousands of years for all that trashed clothing to biodegrade. According to the *New York Times*, "More than 60 percent of fabric fibers are now synthetics, derived from fossil fuels, so if and when our clothing ends up in a landfill...it will not decay....Nor will the synthetic microfibers that end up in the sea, freshwater and elsewhere, including the deepest parts of the oceans and the highest glacier peaks."[6]

Retailer H&M and ad agency AKQA had a mutual *goal*: to change the way we see our old or unwanted clothing—not as waste, but as a resource. They recognized a *gap* in the fashion industry. What if they could recycle people's garments to reduce the burden on landfills? The *gain*: offer H&M customers the opportunity to turn their worn-out clothing into new garments.

Their worthwhile *idea* is Looop, H&M's garment-to-garment recycling system. At the Looop machine, now housed in a glass box designed by Universal, at H&M in central Stockholm, you can select one of eight new, ready-to-wear designs, configured through an app, then watch Looop recycle your old garment into a new one.

"We are constantly exploring new technology and innovations to help transform the fashion industry....Getting customers on board is key to achieve real change, and we are so excited to see what Looop will inspire," said Pascal Brun, head of sustainability at H&M.[7]

Looop was created by the nonprofit H&M Foundation, together with the Hong Kong Research Institute of Textiles and Apparel (HKRITA) and the Hong Kong–based yarn spinner Novetex Textiles. To remake old garments, Looop shreds fabric back into fibers, spins it into yarn, and then knits it into something new, without water or chemicals. "From shirts to skirts and odd socks, old was remade into new, to start a revolution and to help change the way we see fashion, for the better," explains agency AKQA.[8]

The launch of Looop was a huge success. *Fast Company* reported, "H&M will turn your ratty old T-shirt into a brand new sweater."[9] H&M plans to offer Looop at its other stores, and HKRITA, the institute behind the Looop technology, has made the technology available for license to encourage other companies to join the recycling effort.

H&M and AKQA had a *goal* in mind. There was a *gap* in the fashion and recycling industries. The *gain?* Their worthwhile idea is environmentally sustainable.

Why the Three Gs?

So what do Miranda, H&M, and AKQA's idea generation processes have in common? They all can answer probing questions such as, What's my *goal?* Would the outcome of this goal fill a *gap?* Who will *gain* from the outcome?

The Three Gs help you generate, crystallize, or unlock ideas that are worthwhile. Societal value takes many forms. By "worthwhile," I mean ideas of value that make us think critically and creatively, inspire us, or move us the way the arts do; make our lives better; are for the betterment of the world; and consider the triple bottom line—people, the planet, and profit—rather than simply profit or novelty.

Often people convince themselves that good or great ideas require a golden nugget of brilliance (or even genius) possessed by only a fortunate few. Certainly, intelligence refined by education is a key factor. Whether it is to generate a system (think the World Wide Web), invent a product (think Apple iPhone), extend a brand (think Diet Coke), or create a new digital platform (think TikTok), we tend to think an idea must leap fully formed from our heads like Athena did from Zeus. But a golden nugget of genius is not required.

Just about anyone can generate an idea—a hare-brained idea, a poor idea, a meh idea, or a dangerous idea. Many people generate ideas that are corollaries of old ideas. That's not to say that brilliant people don't generate poor ideas; however, they generate many ideas—some that prove worthy of pursuing.

The Three Gs remind us that there is more than one way to generate an idea and direct our energy along the way. Some people start with a *goal* that helps generate ideas. People come to their goals in a variety of ways—because they have a long-standing passion, because their job requires them to respond to a goal, or because they've asked probing questions.

Others might notice a *gap*—a need; a void in a sector, discipline, or subject; an audience who has been underserved or not served at all. When you research a particular field or discipline, you might notice that some areas have not been tapped or have been little explored. It's best to invest your time and resources in an idea that fills a void and moves research or your discipline forward. There's no point in repeating what others have done, unless your only incentive is profit—and even then, imitation can be risky.

Starting on the Path to Worthwhile Ideas

Certain words or phrases can help shed light on pinpointing a *gap*: "the central question remains"; "this has not been brought to light"; "this has not been clarified"; and "it's important to address this lack of knowledge." Ask:

- What issues have people not yet addressed in this field?
- Would I be able to offer a different perspective, one that provides insight?
- Are the methods or procedures in use outdated or no longer considered valid? Is there an alternative method people are reluctant to explore or haven't explored? Is there a way to fill the gap using a cutting-edge approach?
- Is there a zeitgeist to which no one is responding?
- Would collaborating with a person or people from a different discipline, industry, organization, or country offer a fresh perspective and fill a void?
- Would collaborating with a diverse group of people, an inclusive group, offer greater possibilities? Open up the conversation?
- Is there an enduring question that intrigues you? For example, What is good government? What is friendship?

In medical technology, for example, there might be a gap in how insulin is administered or in remotely monitoring a pacemaker device. When researcher Sumita Mitra noticed a gap in the materials used in restorative dentistry, she found that nanomaterials could be used to achieve dental restorations that are durable and aesthetically pleasing, overcoming the limitations of previous dental composites.

In fashion design, there was until recently a *gap* in gender-inclusive apparel for all bodies. Rob Smith founded the Phluid Project in New York City and online. Smith's *goal* was to make gender-free apparel and accessories available worldwide. One objective of the Phluid Project is to challenge the "ethos of dated traditions that inhibit freedom and self-expression, embarking on a mission to improve humanity through not only fashion, but also community outreach, activism, and education."[10] Through his fashion business, Smith has created a more inclusive model, rejecting binary gender norms and allowing people to truly express themselves through fashion, which is a *gain*.

A *goal* and a *gap* that lead to an idea worth pursuing offer a *gain*. Those kinds of ideas are worthwhile, useful, or meaningful for individuals, communities, society, business, creatures big or small, or the planet. They inform, educate, support, empower, elevate, inspire, enrich our creative thinking, move the needle, entertain, advance, provide a utility, or do something for the greater good.

Why can't most people generate worthwhile ideas, even when research and facts are available to them? Generating good new ideas often requires the Three Gs. People generate good ideas when they realize a worthwhile goal, notice the possibilities in a gap or a gain, and ensure all three are working together.

It doesn't matter how creative or daring you are right now. What matters is whether you're open to revising your thinking to seek goals, gaps, and gains to generate great ideas. If you pursue the

Three Gs—this system will accelerate your thinking—you will be on the path to truly worthwhile ideas.

This is the framework behind the New Art of Ideas:

Goal + Gap + Gain → Worthwhile Idea

- What's your *goal*?
- Does your goal fill a *gap*?
- Who will *gain*?

Some people might say your goal is your idea. In fact, it's just the start. Here's why. Without knowing whether your goal fills a gap and produces an actual gain for individuals, society, or our planet, there's no point in pursuing it. That's why you need the Three Gs.

And here's the true beauty of the Three Gs: you can use this framework in any order. A goal isn't always the only entry point for an idea. A gap might be staring you in the face, and you move forward from there. Or you can't help but notice how something is benefiting people—a gain that's so apparent you move ahead from that point. This process is nonlinear. The goal, gap, and gain influence each other—they are synergistic and are not or should not be siloed. The Three Gs also allow you to backtrack and reassess. The Three Gs are fluid.

In the following chapters, I will discuss more about how the Three Gs can play out. But here's an example of a mom who clearly identified a gap and moved forward from there.

During the 1950s, plastics seemed like the future (as noted in a classic reference in the film *The Graduate*, directed by Mike Nichols). Now, however, objects such as plastic shopping bags, which are banned in many places, and single-use plastic sandwich bags contribute to detrimental landfill. While packing lunches for her three children, Kat Nouri noticed this waste.

Nouri wondered, *Why not make a more durable food storage bag that could be used thousands of times instead of just once?* She started not by setting a goal, but by noticing a *gap* in the food storage industry. Nouri then set her *goal* and successfully launched Stasher, a reusable food storage bag, and later sold Stasher to S. C. Johnson.[11] The *gain* is less landfill.

You may spot a gap and a gain simultaneously. Most North American Thanksgiving dinners don't include a main course suitable for vegetarians. Seth Tibbot spent years trying to fill that gap in Thanksgiving dinners so that vegetarians also could enjoy an entrée. Enter Tofurky, a plant-based protein that could serve as a meat-free holiday roast.

Seth Tibbot went from making from-scratch tempeh for friends and family to opening a business selling tempeh, and his mission all along was to bring "efficient, low on the food chain food, to America."[12] With fellow entrepreneurs Hans and Rhonda Wrobel, who owned a vegetarian food company in Portland, Oregon, he formed a partnership. It was Tibbott's idea to borrow and obtain permission to use a name he'd once seen on a tofu sandwich: Tofurky.[13]

Let's look at Tibbott's and the Wrobels' thinking through the lens of the Three Gs. Tibbott had identified a *gap* and a *gain* and formed a *goal*. Together, Tibbott and the Wrobels developed a means to achieve their goal—to produce an entrée that would fill a gap and benefit vegetarians not just at Thanksgiving, but at any lunch or dinner.

Here's how the framework can operate in three iterations. You start with a goal:

Goal + Gap + Gain → Worthwhile Idea

Or you start with a gap:

Gap + Gain + Goal → Worthwhile Idea

Or you start with a gain:

Gain + Gap + Goal → Worthwhile Idea

Now a word about the audience. Those of us in the fields of entrepreneurship, innovation labs, advertising, marketing, communication, journalism, fashion design, communication design, industrial design, interior design, architecture, and interior architecture always think about the people we are serving and at whom we are aiming our ideas. The audience must be paramount in your mind when determining the Three Gs. (I'll cover thinking about your audience in greater depth in chapter 2.)

Who will your idea serve? Who stands to benefit from your idea? Who are you aiming at? Do you have an insight into their behavior or thinking? What do you hope they will think, feel, take away, and do?

For example, if your idea is to design an extremely tall jungle gym because you think children would find it exciting—and they likely would—do you think parents would allow their young children to climb it? I wouldn't. If, however, you design a jungle gym that kids find exciting but that considers all the falls that happen when children climb, you'd be onto something parents would appreciate. Follow the Three Gs—all your good ideas may just surprise you.

🏃 UNLOCK YOUR CREATIVE POTENTIAL 🏃

After reading this chapter, think about how the Three Gs can help you unlock, crystallize, or amplify an idea. Answering these questions is a good place to start:

- Are you responding to a preset goal or taking advantage of an opportunity, a goal you've been dreaming of, or a gap you've noticed?

- Is the goal or the gap worthwhile? How do you know?

- Can you imagine a gain for individuals, society, creatures, or our planet?

Employ the Three Gs to get some answers:

- In your field, what issues have people not yet addressed? For example, Lin-Manuel Miranda filled a gap in Broadway musicals by introducing hip-hop.

- Are the methods or procedures in use outdated or no longer considered valid? Is there an alternative method people are reluctant to explore or haven't explored? Is there a way for you to fill the gap using a cutting-edge approach?

- Is there something in the zeitgeist to which no one is responding?

- Is there an enduring question that intrigues you? For example, What is freedom? What is happiness? Do people hold universal values?

BUILD A CREATIVE HABIT

Creative people train themselves to observe mindfully—to notice what others might miss. To train yourself to be more perceptive, try these exercises:

- Revisit a familiar task, such as brushing your teeth or walking with your dog. Is there anything about the action that you hadn't noticed before?

- Notice people's facial expressions or body language. Really focus on the person you're speaking with or listening to. Do their gestures express something their words are not communicating? (This also will train you to "read" a room if you have to give a presentation. As you observe people's facial expressions, you'll be able to discern whether the audience is attentive to what you're saying.)

- When you take a walk, notice how the shadows fall and the shapes of marks on the sidewalk or road. Observe how people wear scarves, how dancers extend their arms into space. Listen to sounds you might have otherwise ignored, such as leaves rustling or the crumpling of paper. Examine everything anew.

- Observe how someone eats a taco or a sandwich cookie.

In short, notice what others are likely missing.

CHAPTER 2

THE THREE Gs METHOD

*If you find a book you really want to read but it
hasn't been written yet, then you must write it.*
TONI MORRISON

Sal Khan was a successful hedge fund analyst working in Boston
when he learned that his tween cousin Nadia was struggling with
unit conversion in math—a difficulty that was preventing her from
being placed on a more advanced math track at school. "She lived
in New Orleans, so I offered to do distance tutoring with her every
day," said Khan, who has degrees from MIT and Harvard. The tutoring worked. He explained,

> Word soon spread in my family that free tutoring was available,
> and by 2006 I was working with 15 cousins and family friends in my
> limited spare time. I decided to make math practice software and
> videos to help even more. Before I knew it, people who were not
> my cousins started using those materials. Fast-forward to today and
> that family side project has become my life's mission: to provide a
> free, world-class education for anyone, anywhere.[1]

Let's reverse engineer Khan Academy's origin story using the
Three Gs:

Gain + Gap + Goal → Worthwhile Idea

Khan does something for Nadia that works. The consequent *gain* he sees unfolding for his family and others is obvious. He recognizes the *gap*—there is no free tutoring available; there is only expensive tutoring for kids with money and access. So Khan sets a *goal*: building Khan Academy, a tutoring, mentoring, and testing educational organization that offers its content free to anyone with Internet access.

Now he has a fully formed worthwhile idea. There are people who need what his idea has to offer and will absolutely benefit from it. Having difficulty with algebra? Head to Khan Academy. Art history? Chemistry? You know where to go. Anyone can sign up to view the many tutorials, which explain the subjects, and then take the interactive tests. This is the *gain* that Khan clearly saw when so many people wanted his tutoring.

Khan left his corporate career to devote himself to Khan Academy, and if that weren't enough, Khan later set another goal: he partnered with his college friend, Shishir Mehrotra (co-founder and CEO of Coda), to create Schoolhouse.world to provide free, live peer-to-peer tutoring to any student to fill yet another gap in education. In an opinion piece in the *New York Times* about distance learning during the COVID-19 pandemic, Khan wrote about averting an educational catastrophe by doing all we can to ensure that an entire generation of learners is not left with "insurmountable gaps in their education."[2]

When people think of idea generation, they often imagine inventions or business ventures. But ideas are the bedrock of the arts, too. The work of contemporary North American artist Rose Gonnella is held in several major collections, including the Smithsonian American Art Museum (SAAM) and the Sara Roby Foundation Collection. Gonnella works in colored pencil on paper. Two of her works, *Purple Interior with Window*, which depicts a corner of a window and a partial view outside, and the second, *Violet Interior with Lamp*, which depicts a sparsely decorated room, were featured in a recent traveling exhibition, *Modern American Realism: Highlights from the Sara Roby Foundation Collection.*

Gonnella's *goal* for these works was "to transform what we commonly see every day into something more precious."[3] She describes her work as realism with a touch of the surreal: "The drawings are of places I know. But they are not exact places or situations, they are 'memories' and composites."[4] Gonnella told me that one of her gallerists says she "weaves" the drawing with lines of color using pencil. With her distinct technique, she is filling a *gap*. Beyond the uniqueness of her technique, Gonnella's ability to transform an idea into an original visual form transports viewers. Understanding how art fills a gap is somewhat different from perceiving a gap in product design or medicine. You must consider how the art communicates a vision, an idea—how it advances your thinking, unsettles you, challenges you, moves you, advocates, or inspires you. Art's consequences are too great to assign to technique alone.

The *gain?* People who collect Gonnella's work find it thought-provoking and sublime, as do I. Gonnella was the only living artist represented in the *Modern American Realism* exhibit, alongside such renowned artists as Edward Hopper, Isabel Bishop, Stuart Davis, Paul Cadmus, and others.

The Three Gs Method

Let's examine the Three Gs framework when you *start with a goal.*

Set a Goal

Think about what you want to do. Big or small. Invent a new musical instrument. Pivot your business model to a hands-free point-of-sale system. Bake and sell savory spelt scones. (I volunteer to taste-test them.) Reinvent primary education. Generate an idea for the marketing launch of a new product. Design a brand identity. Write "a book you really want to read but it hasn't been written yet." Essentially, a goal is something you are trying to achieve in any field.

In the realm of virtual reality (VR), Israeli fighter pilots Moty Avisar and Alon Geri had a *goal*—giving surgeons the chance to participate in simulated surgery through "a visualization platform that helps to illuminate complex procedures."[5]

"We had an idea," said Avisar, CEO and cofounder of Surgical Theater. "What if surgeons could train like fighter pilots, previewing their surgical procedure like a fighter pilot pre-flying their mission?"[6] Surgical Theater fills a *gap* in surgical practice, and surgeons *gain* experience before they get to operate on people. I would certainly prefer that my surgeon train that way before operating on me.

In the business sphere, Royalty Exchange is a marketplace that allows musical artists to raise funds by selling their royalties to investors during online auctions. "Royalties are the tangible manifestation of these ideas. They are assets that can be bought, sold, and traded. Open markets make assets more valuable by providing transparency, price discovery, and competition needed to satisfy investor demand....Creators can then leverage this demand to find investors for their catalog at the best price possible, raising money without giving up their rights or going into debt," the firm's website explains.[7]

Royalty Exchange's *goal* was to hand some of the financial power of the artists' own ideas back to the artists. The *gap* and the *gain* for artists? No other company provided this service for artists. Anthony Martini, Royalty Exchange's CEO, said, "Royalty Exchange is disrupting the financial landscape of the music business in favor of those who actually create the value in this industry—the artists. That's a mission I can get behind and take to the next level."[8]

Historian Tiya Miles was inspired by an artifact—a photograph of Ashley's sack, sent to her by journalist Ben Goggins—to write *All That She Carried: The Journey of Ashley's Sack, a Black Family Keepsake.*

Miles's *goal?* "I hope *All That She Carried* offers readers many new ways to understand the history of slavery and the experiences of unfree women at that time," she said.[9]

Writing for *Oprah Daily,* Hamilton Cain explains the *gap*:

> Black women and their families have been omitted from the official histories of our country and its archives by many historians. Harvard professor Tiya Miles does wonders in filling those gaps with this sparkling tale of an embroidered bag from 1921. On its surface, Ashley's sack is an intimate family heirloom. In Miles's artful hands, though, the object is transformed—an embodied memoir of Black women traveling from slavery to freedom, South to North, carrying relics and hopes as they seek new lives.[10]

The *gain?* This book takes us on a journey of resilience that, as the publisher says, is an "extraordinary testament to people who are left out of the archives."[11]

Again, please note: Some people might say your *goal* is your idea. But it's only the start. Here's why: Without knowing whether your *goal* fills a *gap* and provides an actual *gain* for individuals, communities, creatures, society, business, or our planet, there's no point in pursuing it. That's why you need the Three G's.

Look for a Gap

Gather information about the subject, problem, or topic. Seek information with an eye toward discovering an *insight*—a void you can fill. Khan realized that there was no free tutoring available to kids in the United States. The insight was that kids needed free academic assistance, beyond the classroom, that they could return to again and again. Hite at Microsoft knew gaming wasn't accessible to all. His insight was that gamers living with disabilities needed a ready-made adaptive controller they could use rather than having to hack a conventional controller. (More about insights to come.)

There are gaps in all fields, and other examples abound. For instance, many digital games are aimed at middle-school boys, but few are aimed at girls of that age; there's a gap in what the gaming industry offers to that demographic audience. Until recently, New York City subway commuters didn't have a live subway map that would show train arrivals and delays. New York's Metropolitan Transit Authority (MTA), the Transit Innovation Partnership, and Work & Co. came together to fill that gap, creating the MTA Live Subway Map. This game-changing map shows daily service in real time, so that riders will know about delays and construction and can manage work-arounds.[12]

Stay open to any enlightening tidbit that points to a potential gap you hadn't anticipated.

When people write academic journal articles, they first do a literature search—a survey of what has been written to identify existing research and find a *gap*, the missing piece or pieces in the discipline, something in the area that has not yet been explored or is underexplored. You're doing something similar (but not necessarily in a formal academic way) to see if your goal will fill a void or address a need that has not yet been met. For example, later in this chapter I'll tell you about paper pill bottles that fill a gap in package design, preventing tons of nonrecyclable toxic waste.

Once you gather information and analyze your data, look for a gap that points to a gain. The *gain* provides a benefit to individuals, a community, society, or our planet in one or more of a whole range of areas. It may entertain, inform, educate, advance commerce, reduce waste, improve quality of life, increase sustainability, provide a utility, support and uplift people, advance a discipline, or do social good. Employing the Three Gs should allow you to generate many good ideas or better ideas.

Here's a helpful tip: Most art directors and designers present more than one ad idea to their creative director or client, making each idea markedly different from the others in the hope that the client will be sold on at least one of the idea directions. There's no point in showing variations on one idea to a creative director or client because it's still only one idea, and if they don't buy into it, you have no backup plan.

How Do You Begin?

If you paid attention to your elementary school science teacher, you might recall the surprising story of the discovery of penicillin—one that surprised Alexander Fleming himself.

When Fleming, a physician and scientist, returned from vacation to his untidy laboratory, he observed something that others might have missed—a mold (called Penicillium) had contaminated one of his petri dishes containing colonies of *Staphylococcus aureus* (a bacteria). Fleming examined the mold and set a *goal*—to determine why it prevented the normal growth of the staphylococci. He went on to experiment and research.

If you've taken an antibiotic to cure an infection, you have Fleming to thank for being alive. When he made his discovery, there was an enormous *gap*—there were no antibiotics. Fleming changed the world of medicine and our lives—an unmitigated *gain* for all. He wrote: "When I woke up just after dawn on September 28, 1928, I certainly didn't plan to revolutionize all medicine by discovering the world's first antibiotic, or bacteria killer. But I guess that was exactly what I did."[13]

Goal

At times, it's simple. Your boss assigns a goal to you, or your own business or project requires a new goal. That determines one G— the *goal*—of the Three Gs. It's a ready-made goal and a problem to solve. If this is the case, first assess the goal. It may be the wrong goal or a result of asking the wrong question! Think critically about it.

Gap

Look for a *gap*. Consider whether to seek a gap in the business model, in the marketing strategy, in the product category, in the industry or sector, in the discipline, in the attention to the audience, and so on.

In some fields, to determine a gap, you must seek an insight into the audience. An *insight* is a realization or revelation about the target audience's need or belief or about their true thoughts, feelings, or behavior—a human truth or finding no one has yet noticed. That insight or human truth ultimately should warrant responsiveness—a change in how you look at a behavior, situation, product, or service—and could be the catalyst for finding a gap. Dove's Real Beauty Campaign, which has been running effectively in various iterations for almost twenty years, used an insight first pointed out by women on the team and later confirmed by extensive research—that "only two percent of women worldwide considered themselves beautiful."[14] That was a powerful sentiment among women that hadn't been addressed before.

You can think of insights in two main ways: A fixed insight dominates what people say and how they behave over an extended period. A dynamic insight bends with small- or large-scale changes in the audience's needs, behavior, or situation—think of a Black Swan event of staggering proportions, such as a pandemic or a hurricane of enormous size and scope.

Creative professionals often use target audiences to get answers to questions and to land on insights:

- Who are you aiming at? Who is the target audience?

- What do they do?

- What's their experience? What influences their experience?

- What's their context for your goal?

- What are their needs?

- What issue does your goal solve for them?

- What would they consider an effective outcome? An outstanding solution?

- What do they stand to gain from using the outcome of this goal?

- What do they think now?

- What are their concerns? Desires?

- What would work for them? What wouldn't?

- What do they feel or think about existing solutions?

- What would you need to communicate to them?

- What actions do you want them to take?

- What would inspire them to act?

Think of an audience *gap* this way: What is missing from their lives? What are their pain points? What would motivate them? Which issues keep them up at night?

How Designers Think about Gaps

When graphic designers and advertising art directors think about gaps, they often think in terms of differentiation. They might think: What's the gap in the marketplace in terms of concept, visualization, and design? How can we differentiate the brand or entity through a design concept and visual design?

Differentiation is what distinguishes one brand or entity from the rest in people's minds, in terms of design concept and visual attributes, such as typeface, color palette, consistent use of imagery, and visualization style or technique. For example, if the main color of the leading brand in a category is red (think Coca-Cola), someone designing a new entry into the category would be unwise to select red, which wouldn't differentiate it.

Differentiating a brand or entity with a distinctive visual identity can establish a brand's essence and fill a gap by ensuring its distinctiveness against its competitors.

How Marketing Professionals Think about Gaps

Marketing professionals also think in terms of differentiation. What position would a brand or entity hold in people's minds? Strong positioning is critical to how a brand or entity exists in the marketplace and in popular culture. Is there a positioning gap in the category?

Is there a gap relative to a brand construct? A brand construct is a theoretical assembly of three main points: what people want and might need in the near future, how the brand fits into what people want and anticipates what they might appreciate, and most important, how the brand's attributes stand out as distinctive in a crowded commercial arena. By creating a construct, the brand or entity stakes a claim—it seeks to "own" a position in the consumer's mind, preempting the competition. ("Own" is in quotes here because most brands do not literally own attributes unless they hold a patent.) People think of that brand related to a claimed attribute or construct. For example, in their market categories, Disney owns family fun and Apple owns creativity. That construct fills a gap in how the brand is positioned in the marketplace.

How Leaders Think about Gaps

Leaders who drive innovation and idea generation are avid gap seekers. They know gaps are where potential lies—for moving a company or discipline forward, addressing a key question, or pursuing an unorthodox path that goes against the conventional wisdom. They also know gaps are where the potential for equity— addressing underserved audiences—lies.

Leaders understand that insights into audiences point toward significant gaps. In a global economy with so many variables, strategically creative leaders tend toward dynamic insights, ones that bend with micro or macro changes in an audience's needs in response to a new behavior (think hours of scrolling or a new platform's draw, such as TikTok challenges), urgent situations (think a tsunami, inflation, a stock market bust, or a war), election results, or a sociopolitical movement. Pinpointing gaps helps leaders understand what's not yet been done so they are prepared to tackle unexpected challenges, can pivot when necessary, and can drive innovation.

Leaders also understand the need for systems. The Three Gs is a fluid ideation system. By seeking gaps, by being aware of paths not taken or paths others won't take, and by identifying underserved audiences and outmoded thinking, the Three Gs can lead to opportunities. Leaders establish practices that allow their organizations to use such systems to create, innovate, and respond to change.

Gain

What is the *gain?* Will achieving the goal and filling the gap make life better, improve society, or improve conditions for individuals, society, business, creatures, or our planet? If you're thinking of profits as the gain, aim toward improving the triple bottom line—profit, people, and the planet. Always keep the people you're aiming at in mind. What can you do to make life better for them?

While worthwhile industrial design and responsible technological ideas move civilization forward, creative gains from art, music, dance, literature, poetry, and film can reveal truths, be vehicles of resistance, make the mundane seem new, and afford insights into ourselves and others. A great work of art reminds us of our humanity.

The following are four examples from my own disciplines, creative advertising and brand experience design, of how being handed a preset goal (a problem to solve) works.

SPOTLIGHT   BURGER KING UK "MELTDOWN"

Burger King's goal in the United Kingdom market was to lead the move away from non-biodegradable plastic toys.

The company worked with creative agency JKR. Katie Evans, marketing director at Burger King UK, said,

> Removing plastic toys from our kids' meals represents a huge
> step for the brand in the UK and we knew we couldn't do this

quietly. The provocative idea that JKR presented demonstrated the engagement we were looking for; we knew it would capture the nation's attention and change kids' meals forever. This is an opportunity for us to lead radical change in our industry and we know we can positively contribute to finding new, more sustainable solutions, long term.[15]

Burger King set the *goal* for JKR: find a way to remove plastic toys.

Inspired by Burger King's irreverent spirit, JKR realized the *gain*: Burger King is melting down plastic toys to upcycle them into something useful and fun for kids. "It's brilliant that these toys will be transformed into play areas and playful experiences that last longer than a few minutes," explained Stephen McDavid, creative director at JKR.[16] The *gap*? Interactive play opportunities for families at Burger King restaurants.

What did they do? They asked parents and kids to bring their unwanted plastic toys to a BK restaurant for a "meltdown" so the toys could be recycled into interactive play opportunities. The Meltdown saved 320 tons of plastic and made recycling fun for BK's youngest customers.

SPOTLIGHT   LISA SMITH / CHOBANI REBRAND

When Leland Maschmeyer was the chief creative officer at Chobani, he recruited Lisa Smith to join the in-house creative team to rebrand the visual identity. According to *Fast Company*, Maschmeyer "wanted the identity to have a sense of romance, nature, and the craftsmanship inspired by Northeastern American folk art." And he focused on a phrase as a kind of brand essence: "Happily ever after."[17]

Smith reworked the phrase to "Fighting for happily ever after" after reading a story about Chobani's founder, Hamdi Ulukaya, in

Fast Company, where Ulukaya talked about being a "shepherd of delicious, accessible, and nutritious food, and a warrior for ethical food practices."

The *gap?* "We talked a lot about *compassionate power*, and those were words I could turn into design," Smith says.

The *gain?* "Smith and her team weren't branding a product; they were building a world. According to Maschmeyer, they overhauled the brand identity, website, café, and packaging, and expanded products like the Flip, a yogurt that has toppings consumers dump on top."[18]

Armin Vit, critic at *Brand New*, called the new identity "literally and absolutely perfect."[19]

Designers start with a design or creative brief, which might or might not state the goal. If the brief doesn't include one, you need to determine the goal based on the information provided in the brief, as well as any additional research or information you can gather on your own.

Then it's up to you and your colleagues on the creative team to figure out the gap and gain. At times, the brief will provide research on the marketplace and competition, which might inform you about a possible gap. The brief also might provide information about the target audience, which could help you come up with a possible desirable gain for the audience. Ask, What's in it for them?

When you respond to a creative brief, the gap you identify needs to address the goal, of course, and the target audience's needs and desires. What is missing from their lives? What are their pain points? This gap might not be that different from other gaps, but you must focus on the people the brief specifies.

The Three Gs work extremely well in concert with design briefs and creative briefs!

Here's some Alexander Hamilton trivia: they say Aaron Burr wrote his duel challenge to Hamilton on paper made by Crane, a company that has been manufacturing paper in the United States for more than 250 years. Recently, the brand experience design company Collins revitalized the Crane brand. Collins's *goal* was to reboot the brand's digital presence, develop a more relevant brand voice, and enable new products, artist collaborations, and customization capabilities.

Collins sees Crane as filling a *gap*: "What will you make worth keeping?" In today's digital world, Crane's paper products enable you to express yourself with thoughtfulness and permanence. The designers also drew inspiration from Crane's history, making the imagery and essence unique to the brand. "Human beings throughout history have found significance through connection....When the world is burning, we look to nature to restore and repair our damages. When we're searching for intimacy, we put our phones away and look at each other face to face. When we want to be heard and remembered, we write a letter," notes Collins' website.[20]

The *gain* is a humanistic tool for expression and communication. "The idea was to create objects of desire," Nick Ace, a creative director at Collins, said about the studio's work on Crane's products and its approach to the brand identity. "The Crane box should never be hidden in a drawer or tossed in a closet. It should be proudly displayed on your desk, your shelf or on your coffee table. Its tactile qualities should make you want to touch it—intrigue you to open it up to see what's inside."[21]

Before we move on to goals that are not preset, there's something important to understand. A goal can be broken down into objectives. To see how, let's go back to the Burger King (BK) brand and an award-winning marketing campaign by FCB New York, "The Whopper Detour."

◉ SPOTLIGHT BURGER KING "THE WHOPPER DETOUR"

The BK *goal* for this marketing effort was to get people to use mobile ordering. FCB broke that goal into three main corporate objectives: (1) create top-of-mind awareness of Burger King's app, (2) get people to download the app, and (3) get people to actually use the app. A case study write-up explains:

> BK needed to generate excitement for its revamped mobile app
> with order-ahead functionality. Rather than using a typical coupon,
> we leveraged a powerful insight: With the new BK App, anywhere
> can be a place to order a Whopper—even a McDonald's, turning
> their much larger footprint into ours. Rewarding customers
> with a $0.01 Whopper (when ordered from McD's), we invited
> consumers to engage in the trolling fun, hitting #1 on both app
> stores, generating 1.5 million downloads in just 9 days, and an ROI
> of 37:1.[22]

What was the *gap?* Well, it wasn't the app, which was basic. Rather, the gap was giving young people an opportunity to participate in an outrageous troll against a rival. The *gain?* A $0.01 Whopper (when ordered within 600 feet of a McD's) and trolling fun for the audience.

The worthwhile *idea:* Buy a Whopper for just one cent. The catch: Customers could order it only on the Burger King app "at" McDonald's.

Ways into the Three Gs

When there are no preset goals, demands, or guidelines, let's look at ways you can use the Three Gs to generate, crystallize, or amplify worthwhile ideas.

Build on an Observation

Keen observation is fundamental to scientific research, as it is to so many disciplines. Once Alexander Fleming observed the curious mold, he set a *goal*. For his discovery of *Penicillium*, he earned a Nobel Prize. As Aria Nouri points out in her article "*Penicillium* and the Importance of Observation," Fleming observed with a prepared mind and a keen eye, he was deeply curious, and he translated observation into meaningful results.[23] There are many ways to set a goal. At times, you happen on it, as did Fleming and Khan. But they only happened on their goals because their minds were intellectually alert and prepared to notice possibilities.

We're so used to grabbing an iced latte or a cup of coffee at Starbucks that people are surprised to learn that Starbucks originally did not sell individual cups of brewed coffee. In their first stores in Seattle, you could purchase fresh-roasted coffee beans, tea, and spices to take home. When the marketing director of Starbucks, Howard Schultz, first visited Milan, he observed the Italian café model. "The Italians had created the theater, romance, art and magic of experiencing espresso," Schultz recalled. "I was overwhelmed with a gut instinct that this is what we should be doing."[24]

Schultz came back with an idea sparked by watching the Italian baristas in Milan's coffee houses, which he presented to the owners of Starbucks Coffee Company. But the Starbucks founders disagreed with Schultz. When Schultz finally purchased Starbucks from them, he turned it into the café we know today. Schultz started with an observation. He knew the United States didn't have the kind of coffee house he observed in Italy—there was a *gap* in the U.S. marketplace.

Schultz's *goal* was to fill the *gap* with the Italian model he fell in love with. The *gain* is clear when you see how many people drink their brew and enjoy the café environment.

The Starbucks story offers a lesson: If you notice a gap, investigate. Find out if there is a need to fill that void. Determine what the gain would be and how many people it would serve.

An observation doesn't have to be one that sets a goal in motion. You may observe a gap or a gain and start from there.

As a professor, I have noticed over the years that my students prefer to listen to my lectures and actively participate rather than take notes. At the same time, I would like to be able to hand over all I know about a subject to them. I thought it would benefit my students to have a reference—all my lessons in one handy resource—which would be the *gain*. So I searched to see if any book existed that provides all I provide on the subject. Sure enough, there were gaps—no books covered idea generation, design, and art direction. My goal: to write books about graphic design and creative advertising. The result is my books *Graphic Design Solutions*, now in its sixth edition, and *Advertising by Design*, in its fourth edition, both translated into Spanish and Chinese.

The lesson: I noticed a pattern of student behavior that led me to think of a *gain*, conducted research to see if a *gap* existed, and coupled it with my expertise, which helped me form a *goal*.

Spot a Problem That Needs Fixing

You're in a unique position to see a problem that needs fixing.

When Sam Farber saw that his wife's arthritis made it difficult for her to use an ordinary vegetable peeler for food preparation, he thought there must be a way to produce kitchen tools that work for everyone. Farber noticed a pain point—a problem that could be fixed through better design. By observing his wife's struggle, Farber realized the *gap* in product design. With that, he saw an opportunity to improve a product—a *gain* for people, which became his *goal.*

"At OXO, we look at everyday objects and activities and we see ways to make things simpler, easier, more thoughtfully designed— better," notes the OXO company website. "We notice things. We notice pain points and pains-in-the-neck. We notice problems people don't realize are problems until we solve them. We see opportunities to improve a product or a process, or a part of everyday life, and we make things that make things better."[25]

Here's another example from my own life that shows that anyone—a parent, a grandparent, a tinkerer—can effectively use the Three Gs to solve a problem. After my three-year-old daughter, Hayley, had two nights of bad dreams resulting in significant sleep disturbance and distress for her, my husband, and myself, I had a problem to solve—a goal. I conducted casual research about children's nightmares. Johns Hopkins Medicine suggested, among other things, comforting, reassuring, and cuddling your child and leaving the child's bedroom door open, all of which I did.[26] Easy enough.

Then I thought of my own experience: when I'm upset about something, I compartmentalize my emotions—put them away, as if in a drawer—in order to concentrate when I'm teaching, writing, or consulting. That sparked the Dream Box.

"This is a Dream Box," I said to Hayley, as I opened a tea box I had covered with wrapping paper. "Tell your nightmare to this Dream Box. Then close the lid, and I'll put the Dream Box away. You won't have any more bad dreams."

Hayley did as I asked. She then said, "How does it work?"

"It's magic. It just does."

At Hayley's age, magical thinking works. Young children believe in magical notions such as the Tooth Fairy. The Dream Box idea worked for Hayley, so I wanted to turn it into a children's book to help other families. To make sure I was on the right track, I spoke with a prominent psychologist, who said she advises her clients to write bad thoughts down and put them in a drawer or throw them away. (Years later, I read a paper with a similar thesis published in the journal *Psychological Science*.[27]) Disguised as a picture book, *The Dream Box* helps solve a common real-life dilemma—what to do when a child has a bad dream.

My *goal*: Stop Hayley's bad dreams. The *gap*: No device existed at the time. The *gain*: We all got some sleep.

Now my friend the psychologist uses *The Dream Box* in her practice. Many parents have written to thank me for this book and useful device. (The nicest part is that they send lovely photos of their children holding the book with their notes.)

We face so many neglected problems in so many sectors. There is always a need for new worthwhile ideas, and there's always been a need for urgent ideas during times of war, famine, pandemic, typhoon, or other acts of nature or human-caused disasters.

You could think of a *gap* as a neglected problem. For instance, because they're small, plastic pill bottles cannot be recycled—they become toxic waste.

Notice Pain Points

To ensure user-friendly design, product developers, web developers, and user-experience designers need to notice pain points. If you search social media to see what people are complaining about—what their pain points are on various topics, products, services, and brands—you might get an insight into setting a goal, filling a gap, or providing a gain.

One pain point for many in the LGBTQIA+ community is the extra scrutiny, risk, or embarrassment that can come with using a credit or debit card that shows their birth name or deadname rather than their preferred name—their true name. To fix this pain point, Mastercard took a step to empower transgender and nonbinary cardholders. Mastercard explains, "We worked to ease this pain point by creating True Name, a first-of-its-kind feature that makes secure payments truly safe for all."[28]

The *goal* of the True Name initiative was to allow people to use their chosen name on their Mastercard and to get banks on board—which they did. This filled a *gap* in the credit sector and alleviated a pain point in the LGBTQIA+ community. The *gain?* Mastercard's allyship marks a significant, large-scale corporate commitment to the LGBTQIA+ community, one that will make people's daily lives a little easier.

Another way to bring attention to a pain point is to ask, How can I make an existing product or service more accessible? For many people living with disabilities, lacing up athletic shoes is difficult. Sarah Reinertsen, who has set marathon records and represented the United States at the Paralympic Games, works at Nike. She set a goal of producing a hands-free shoe and was on the team that launched the Nike Go FlyEase.

Tobie Hatfield, senior director of athlete innovation at Nike, had designed a (provisional) shoe for a Nike colleague who had suffered a stroke, which made tying his shoes no longer possible. Then, a letter arrived. According to *Bloomberg,*

> The focus on ease of use coalesced in 2012, when Hatfield read
> a letter from a teenager with cerebral palsy who wanted to be
> self-sufficient but couldn't tie his shoes. Three years later the first
> FlyEase hit the market in the form of a LeBron James high-top that
> used a wraparound zipper to open up the rear of the shoe. The
> latest model took years to develop.[29]

A hinge in the middle of the Nike Go FlyEase, launched in 2021, allows the shoe to bend open, allowing people to slip it on and off with no hands. A midsole tensioner band, made from surgical tubing, snaps the shoe back into place.

So, what do the Mastercard's True Name initiative and Nike's Go FlyEase shoe idea generation processes have in common?

What starts with thinking about a pain point for a specific audience accumulates into something much more when you ask probing questions, such as, What's my *goal?* What needs fixing? Would the outcome of this goal fill a *gap?* Who will *gain* from the outcome? How can I make life better for this audience?

So many of people's worthwhile goals stem from issues in their lives or the lives of people close to them, which leads them to investigate possible solutions.

Follow a Passion

Many worthwhile ideas stem from people's passions—their interest in a subject, a hobby, something they do beyond their job, or something they just keep at until it works. When you're thinking about something you love, it doesn't seem like work. In fact, it is enthralling.

Brother and sister Ahmed Rahim and Reem Hassani had a goal— to bring the dried lime tea they enjoyed during their childhood in Baghdad, Iraq, to the United States. They believe in the healing power of tea. They named their company Numi (*numi* means "citrus" in Arabic); the tea symbolizes hospitality and community. With so many tea brands already available in the United States, what gap have this passionate duo filled? Not only have Rahim and Hassani introduced little-known herbs and teas to the United States, but they are advancing human rights around the globe. There are multiple gains from their business, which brings clean drinking water and sanitation to tea-farming communities, ensures fair wages and safe working conditions, benefits the communities of the farmers who grow the tea, and reduces plastic waste, among other sustainable outcomes. Their passion and vision drove their *goal*; they saw a *gap* and achieved several *gains*.

Go with What You Know Best

Sometimes you can apply the Three Gs to what's right in front of you, to what you know best. Having worked for several leading financial institutions, Gaurav Sharma saw how hard it is for most people to understand their retirement accounts. He decided to build a company that makes it easier. With Chris Phillips, he cofounded Capitalize. When you change jobs, Capitalize will manage your 401(k) rollover for you so you don't lose your money. Like Capitalize, your idea can be a straightforward solution.

Do What Makes Sense for Your Company's
Plan, Customers, and Our Planet

The U.S. Environmental Protection Agency (EPA) considers furniture municipal solid waste. Although some percentage of furniture and furnishings are combusted for energy recovery, most of these products are discarded and end up in landfill.[30] This means that millions of pieces of secondhand furniture go to waste each year.

Recognizing this gap in recycling, Ikea is giving new life to chairs, shelves, and chests of drawers with its buyback and resell service—from "pre-loved" to "re-loved." To reach its *goal* of being a fully circular business, Ikea creates "products that can be used and re-used for many years to come, right up until it's time to recycle them and start again."[31]

The *gain?* Ikea wants to be "100% circular and have a positive impact on the environment. That means not only rethinking the materials we use and the design from the outset, but also providing services to extend the life of our products as much as possible."[32] Through reuse and recycling, Ikea and its customers reduce waste.

The *gap?* There are stores that sell refurbished or refinished furniture, but most companies that manufacture and sell new furniture don't offer to buy back used furniture for reuse or recycling. Ikea filled both marketing and sustainability gaps.

Ask Yourself What You Wish Existed in the World
(or "What's Missing?")

We have all seen and heard stories of people suffering from mental health issues, yet resources for help are scarce, especially in times of national or economic crisis. Ariela Safira started Real, a mental health care company with a new therapy model, when a close friend attempted suicide. Safira identified a glaring *gap*: many people believe mental health care is out of reach. It is for people with more money, better insurance, or perhaps worse symptoms. Her *goal* was to offer therapy at a reasonable rate, making it accessible to all. Real offers a digital membership for $28 a month, which gives members access to a suite of mental health products and services.

The *gain*? Safira is rethinking the mental health care system to create a model that meets people's needs at all levels.

SPOTLIGHT THE PRESCRIPTION PAPER PILL BOTTLE

When plastic pill bottles tumbled out of his medicine cabinet one day, Scott Carlton, a creative director at Saatchi & Saatchi Wellness, wondered, *What happens to these bottles when they're tossed away?* "After conducting research, his creative team learned that most plastic pill bottles cannot be properly disposed of because of their small size," Lillianna Vazquez, group art supervisor, Saatchi & Saatchi Wellness, told me. "That sparked the idea: Create a 100% compostable and biodegradable alternative."

This new bottle meets FDA requirements for water, light, and child resistance. Once emptied, it can be composted to enrich the soil, giving back to the earth. It is a reusable, sustainable container. No plastic. No artificial glue and coatings. No toxic dyes.

According to Carlton, "Made in partnership with TOM, Tikkun Olam Makers, the global maker group dedicated to creating affordable solutions for neglected problems, the paper pill bottle has an open-sourced design available to any pharmacy. And produced bottles have been distributed to local pharmacies for trial."[33]

I am particularly proud to write about this idea because Lillianna Vazquez, who was on the creative team for this project at Saatchi

& Saatchi Wellness, was my student at Kean University. For this creative idea and solution, the agency won a Cannes Lions award.

We can reverse engineer their thinking to see it this way: The *gain* was a compostable and biodegradable pill bottle. The *gap* was an alternative to plastic for pill bottles. The *goal* was to manufacture a 100% compostable prescription pill bottle made of paper.

Ask, "What Else?"

When you're observant, what you see, hear, notice, or investigate might trigger a goal. Take George de Mestral. You might not recognize his name, but you've heard of Velcro, a combination of "velvet" and "crochet" (which means "hook" in French). While walking in the woods, de Mestral noticed that his pants and his Irish Pointer's hair were covered in burs from a burdock plant. Curious, he studied the burs under a microscope to realize that they bind themselves to almost any fabric, even to dog hair. "His idea was to take the hooks he had seen in the burs and combine them with simple loops of fabric. The tiny hooks would catch in the loops, and things would just, well, come together."[34]

De Mestral's keen observational skills led him to the goal of creating a synthetic fabric that would offer a new way to fasten things.

If you work as a creative professional in an advertising agency, you must generate many ideas daily. If you work as a graphic designer, industrial designer, environmental designer, architect, or fashion designer, it is likely that you must do the same. And although you may have learned to ideate in college, it's challenging to generate many quality ideas daily. That's why it's so important to be observant, to notice potential and possibilities.

Professionals in business, marketing, journalism, engineering, communications, entrepreneurship and innovation, media, TV and film, strategy, and many other fields must generate ideas on a regular basis. Sometimes they have preset goals, and other times they must set their own goals.

Some goal seekers are on the lookout for how they can alter an existing idea by adding a creative twist, such as with Schultz and Starbucks. Other goal-prone thinkers train themselves to be on the lookout for pain points—a persistent problem with a product or service that annoys people or is bad for the planet, such as plastic pill bottles. I'll end this chapter with advice from a scientist I admire greatly, not only for his brilliance but for his humanity: Albert Szent-Györgyi, a Hungarian-born biochemist and anti-fascist activist who received the Nobel Prize in 1937 and a Lasker Award in 1954. "Think boldly," Szent-Györgyi said, "don't be afraid of making mistakes, don't miss small details, keep your eyes open, and be modest in everything except your aims."[35] This was Szent-Györgyi's advice to his biographer, Ralph Moss.

UNLOCK YOUR CREATIVE POTENTIAL

After completing this chapter, here are your action steps:

Think about your goal, a gap you've noticed, or a gain you'd like to see in the world. Use the Three Gs to unlock your creativity:

- Do you have a goal in mind?

- Have you noticed or researched a gap in a field or discipline?

- Would your idea offer a benefit, a gain to individuals, society, or our planet?

More specifically related to this chapter:

- Has someone asked you to help them with something because of your expertise? (think Sal Khan and Khan Academy)

- Have you observed a promising business model that is missing in your neck of the woods? (think Howard Schultz and Starbucks)

- Have you noticed anything in your household and wondered what its lifecycle is? (think Saatchi & Saatchi Wellness and the paper pill bottle)

- Have you ever thought about a marketing solution that the target audience would find participatory and fun? (think FCB and Burger King's "Whopper Detour")

BUILD A CREATIVE HABIT

Being curious, as a matter of course, opens your mind to new knowledge and to questions that might unlock idea-producing insights or gaps. Think of how curious George de Mestral was about the burs from a plant sticking to his pants, which led to his idea for Velcro.

Curiosity compels you to learn all you can about your discipline and to keep learning about it. After all, to become an expert at something, you must keep learning and practicing. Curiosity also compels people to learn about different subjects. Just think of Lin-Manuel Miranda picking up a book about Alexander Hamilton to read while on vacation.

Curiosity is a form of information seeking to gain knowledge and improve cognition—thinking processes by which you accumulate knowledge that can help you recognize, perceive, and conceive ideas.

As Albert Einstein said, "I have no special talents. I am only passionately curious."

NOTES: YOUR IDEAS

Is there something you've always wanted to do, accomplish, or create–something that might genuinely make a difference in people's lives?

CHAPTER 3

GOAL

It's the idea that matters. It doesn't matter where you come
from or what your background is. One revolutionary idea,
one brilliant invention can unleash other entrepreneurs to
revolutionize industries in ways you can never predict.
SUNDAR PICHAI, CEO, ALPHABET (GOOGLE)

A few years ago, Alexandra Dean told me about *Bombshell: The Hedy Lamarr Story,* a documentary Dean and producer Adam Haggiag were working on. As a film buff, I knew Hedy Lamarr was a glamorous Hollywood film star and Austrian Jewish immigrant, but I didn't know Lamarr was also an ingenious inventor, a pioneer in modern communications technology.

In 1937 Lamarr left her husband, an Austrian weapons manufacturer. At dinner parties during her marriage, Lamarr had heard her husband's business associates talk about building weapons and developing detection devices to listen to and jam American aircraft radio signals.

Lamarr wanted to short-circuit their plans.

In the early years of World War II, Lamarr had a clear *goal:* to invent a device to block enemy ships from jamming U.S. torpedo guidance signals. She met and began working with George Antheil, a composer who shared her interest in invention, to create a device to achieve Lamarr's goal. "They found a way for the radio guidance transmitter and the torpedo's receiver to jump simultaneously from frequency to frequency, making it impossible for the enemy to locate and block a message before it had moved to another frequency. This approach became known as 'frequency hopping,'" Alice George explains in *Smithsonian Magazine*.[1] Their technique for spread-spectrum communications would become the basis for Bluetooth, GPS, and Wi-Fi technologies.

Lamarr had always had an interest in how things work—at the age of five, she dismantled a music box and reassembled it. She never lost that childhood aptitude for invention and passionate curiosity that fueled her goals. So when an urgent purpose arose, Lamarr set her goal.

When setting a goal, you don't need to clearly articulate the goal, as Lamarr did, for your thinking process to begin. You can start by noticing an opportunity or asking questions.

All professors hope what they say will change their students' lives for the better. While giving a lecture on sustainability, Alan Ross, a professor of business ethics at the University of California, Berkeley, randomly mentioned that gourmet mushrooms can grow on spent coffee grounds.

Two Berkeley seniors, Alejandro Velez and Nikhil Arora, each reached out separately to Ross to find out more. Ross connected Velez and Arora, and the two hit it off. Not only had the mushroom factoid piqued their interest, but they also wanted to learn how other foods grow. After the two grew a first crop of mushrooms during their last semester, the Berkeley chancellor awarded them a $5,000 grant. Though they didn't know much about farming, the pair decided not to pursue corporate business careers in favor of a new *goal*: becoming urban farmers in Oakland, California. They learned what they needed by watching YouTube videos and trial and error.

To house their urban farm, they rented a warehouse near the

airport. They collected spent coffee grounds from Berkeley and Oakland cafés and used them as a growing medium for their mushrooms, which they sold to the local Whole Foods and other stores. Unlike many startups, they made a profit right off. Talking about their business process with host Guy Raz on the NPR podcast *How I Built This*, Velez and Arora explained that cafés actually paid them to haul away the used coffee grounds, stores paid for the mushrooms grown on the coffee grounds, and other customers paid them for the nutrient-rich coffee soil the mushrooms grew on.[2] What started out as a homegrown experiment had turned into a successful business.

But the farming duo shifted gears and set a new *goal*: to "undo food." They stopped growing mushrooms and started a home organic gardening business, Back to the Roots, selling tabletop grow kits, seeds, and potting soil, which now boasts $100 million in sales. Its products are sold in more than 14,000 stores worldwide, including Whole Foods, Costco, and Nordstrom. And because they care deeply that children understand there is an alternative to processed food, Velez and Arora formed a partnership with food product supplier Sodexo to develop a presence in more than 3,000 schools across the United States. They are on a mission to reconnect families and children to where food comes from by helping them grow it themselves—"no green thumb or backyard needed." Cofounder and co-CEO Velez said that they're seeing a great deal of interest from families who want to experience food this way. The seed of a college project has grown into a national brand.

Ask, "What If?"

What if? is a magical question. It invites you to speculate, to wonder. It's a helpful tool for forming a goal if you don't have one at the start. Any probing question—such as "If only…" and "I wonder…"—works to seed ideas, foster a creative mindset, determine goals, and in turn raise other questions. These types of questions foster imaginative and unconventional avenues of thought. On his website, author Neil Gaiman advises, "You get ideas when you ask yourself simple questions. The most important of the questions is just, What if…?"[3]

Here are a few examples to demonstrate how you can speculate to pin down a goal:

What if…

- there were a tool that allowed the world to collaborate from home? (think Zoom)
- we could remotely check pacemakers using our smartphones? (think MyCareLink Heart mobile app)
- we could book a commercial flight to outer space on a rocketship? (think SpaceX)
- we could have grid-free electricity? (think Reeddi, a compact and portable solar-powered battery)
- we valued digital art in a whole new way? (think NFTs [worthwhile for our planet?])

You know the answers to these what-if questions because people set them as goals and then went on to realize them.

The Canadian Down Syndrome Society and Google asked their own what-if question: What if voice technology could be trained in a specific way? Their goal: making voice assistants more accessible.

SPOTLIGHT   CDSS / PROJECT UNDERSTOOD

If you've ever used voice-assisted technology, you know it can be tricky. Although all of the kinks in this technology have not yet been worked it out, we will be relying on it more and more; soon there will be billions of voice assistants.[4]

But if the future is voice-first, does it include everyone? For people living with Down syndrome, voice-assisted technology could be extremely useful, allowing them to live more independently by doing everything from providing appointment reminders to offering directions on how to do things. However, although technologies using voice commands are becoming commonplace, they aren't trained to understand people with Down syndrome and others with atypical speech patterns.

The Canadian Down Syndrome Society (CDSS) and ad agency FCB Toronto saw the gap in voice-assisted technology—it wasn't inclusive and therefore not equitable. They asked, What if we could make voice assistants more accessible? Not only would there be a gain for people living with Down syndrome, but the technology would eventually benefit others with different forms of atypical speech.

The goal of the CDSS and FCB was to ensure that voice-assisted technology would serve people living with Down syndrome. Once they decided to pursue their goal, they realized they needed support and partnered with Google.[5] The *idea* was to teach Google's voice-assisted technology to recognize voice commands from people with Down syndrome.

The CDSS explains that machines learn through data. Having more data certainly increases the accuracy of the machine. "To teach voice technology, the data we need are voice recordings.... The more voice samples shared by the Down syndrome community, the closer we get to a world where every person is understood."[6]

CDSS and Google asked people with Down syndrome to donate their voices. People could fill out a form, log in with Google, and start recording phrases. They were asked to recruit others. Because not all human speech is the same, each voice added helped Google's artificial intelligence technology better understand. "By read-ing and recording simple phrases, we can help Google recognize your unique speech patterns to improve Google's system. Your voice recordings will be used for the purpose of research, with the goal to ultimately improve the accuracy of speech recognition for people with Down syndrome."[7]

The *gain* beyond that? "By sharing their voices with Google, people with Down syndrome are becoming the teachers," said FCB chief creative officer Nancy Crimi-Lamanna. "They're not only taking the lead on helping to ensure a more accessible future for people with Down syndrome, but in the process, demonstrating just how capable they are by teaching Google, one of the smartest technologies on earth."[8]

FCB's website noted, "Though people with Down syndrome are often associated with needing help, the campaign flips the stereo-type around and turns them into the helpers."[9]

Project Understood is a worthwhile idea. The CDSS and FCB asked "What if" to ensure that people with Down syndrome are supported within society and treated and portrayed with respect.

Let's look at Project Understood thinking through the lens of the Three Gs. The CDSS recognized the *gap* in voice-assisted technology for people with Down syndrome. They understood the incredible *gain* for this community if Google's voice-assisted tech-nology were accessible. So the CDSS and FCB Toronto set a *goal* of teaching Google's voice-assisted technology to recognize voice commands by people living with Down syndrome.

Challenge the Status Quo

If you are still unsure of your goal, try this—challenge the status quo.

When I started teaching, I suggested revising teaching methods to a more active model as a way of better reaching different types of learners and engaging all students. The response from senior colleagues was, "Well, we've always done it this way."

I've heard that before, and I'm sure you've heard people say it at work or even at home. Any entrenched mindset fights finding a novel approach. Entrenchment happens when a belief or way of doing something becomes so firmly set that it becomes part of a person's identity or corporate or organizational culture. When this happens, there often is resistance to changing the status quo. Resisting the status quo helps unlock creative potential.

Just because something has been done one way for a long time doesn't mean it's the only way or the right way. People have always enjoyed browsing bookshops and buying books in brick-and-mortar shops. Many would not have believed we would be amenable to buying books online. The big networks traditionally released television programs incrementally. Someone realized people might enjoy binge-watching the entire season of a series. Only thirty years ago, few people shopped via catalog—most preferred to shop in person. Now, online shopping for groceries, electronics, and even cars is a given.

By thinking differently from prevailing conventions, you might discover a goal. Ask yourself, What type of method might be disruptive? New? Not preconceived? Rebellious? Ask a bold or dissenting question.

Challenging the status quo usually means you're employing unconventional thinking. Your goal might go against prevailing public or professional opinion, against the Star Chamber. Mavericks often conceive ideas that might seem radical or ridiculous to conventional thinkers. And what's worse, most companies and even schools expect and reward pedestrian thinking to solve problems, relying on established constructs, techniques, methodologies, and practices. This is where you must be brave.

Take Sara Blakely, the founder and owner of the shapewear brand SPANX. She was getting dressed to attend a party when she realized she didn't have the right undergarment to present the look she wanted. Using her ingenuity, she cut the feet off of her control-top pantyhose to serve as the desired "compression" undergarment. That was the catalyst for SPANX. I'm telling you this story because Blakely is an unconventional thinker. However, she decided not to tell her idea to anyone close to her because she didn't want to hear "That won't work." Conventional thinkers often don't get unconventional thinking. Blakely set a goal and didn't want to be dissuaded from achieving it.

You've likely heard about established academies balking at new ideas from people who go on to be innovators (think of the critics' reactions to Claude Monet's *Impression, Sunrise* or Richard Rogers and Renzo Piano's Pompidou Center; even the practice of hand-washing by physicians advocated by Ignaz Semmelweis [in 1846 Vienna] was once controversial). Conventional thinking is thinking within an existing construct or model. Unconventional thinking may follow creative lines of thought that tend to generate original solutions.

Another way to think about pinpointing a goal is to determine a wrong goal. "Business as usual." "This is the way things are." "It worked for them so it will work for us." So many people in leadership positions emphasize the "right" methodology or goal. Thinking of the wrong goal leads you away from pedestrian ones or ones that don't offer a gain. To combat complacency and same-old thinking, think wrong.

This method works in two ways. C-suite folks often ask, "How can we make what we do better?" Reverse that. Rephrase the question to solicit this goal: "How can we make it worse?" Conceiving the worst solution might inform your thinking or assessment of what people really want. For instance, instead of asking "How can we get more people to subscribe to our evening dress rental service?" ask "How can we get people to unsubscribe?" Illuminating pain points can lead you to ways to improve a service or product, and that improvement becomes a goal.

If you're trying to improve a food delivery service, for instance, think of all the ways you could get it wrong—all the issues that would annoy people. Late deliveries. Cold food. Wasteful packaging. Rude staff. Chronic delays. Exorbitant service fees. And so on. This way of thinking can help you see what the right goal would be.

Another way this approach works is to set a pedestrian goal, one that has been done before or is painfully dull. If you're conceiving and designing an advertisement for a brand of facial tissues, a pedestrian goal would be to make sure people notice the brand name by slapping a big picture of the tissue package in the center of the ad or making the logo huge. Seeing the product in that way immediately signals: This is an ad. Who wants to engage with something that's clearly trying to sell a common commodity to you? Besides, that's a boring solution—it's not going to engage or attract anyone except the brand manager. Thinking of wrong or pedestrian solutions prompts you to think of a goal, and ultimately an idea, that would be more engaging and might get under people's advertising radar.

Maybe that's not how you think, which is just fine. There are plenty of ways to pinpoint an original goal. As I mentioned earlier, a passion of yours might be your way in.

Follow a Passion

If you've ever wondered why Instagram's original image formats were square rather than the conventional rectangular shape of most photographs, the answer lies with Instagram cofounder Kevin Systrom's experience. When he was a Stanford University student, he studied abroad in Italy, where he brought with him his love of photography and a high-quality camera. His professor in Italy suggested ditching his high-quality camera in favor of a Holga film camera, an inexpensive one that takes square, somewhat distressed-looking (or vintage-style) photos. Systrom agreed and grew to appreciate Holga's photo quality.

Systrom is also a bourbon aficionado. Years after his college graduation and work experience in tech companies, he created a location-based iPhone app—his first tech solo enterprise—called Burbn, which allowed users to check in at particular locations, make plans for future check-ins, earn points for hanging out with friends, and post pictures of their meetups.

Burbn wasn't a hit, but Systrom kept tweaking the app, paying close attention to how people were using it. He brought on another programmer, Mike Krieger, and the pair used analytics to determine exactly how their customers were using Burbn. Their findings? People weren't using Burbn's check-in features at all. What they were using were the app's photo-sharing features.[10]

After analyzing their data and realizing people were enthusiastically posting and sharing photos, Systrom and Krieger focused on just that—a photo-sharing app we know as Instagram.

Systrom's love of photography and bourbon fueled his goal.

What are you passionate about? If you love soccer, hiking with friends, or curating fashion, could you determine a goal based on one of your passions? Many people form goals out of an unbridled interest in a subject, activity, or combo of things. An attorney friend had a general goal for her early retirement—she wanted to focus on creative activities. She had always wanted to use her love of art, design, and fashion as the basis for her career, but her pragmatism won out; she became an attorney.

Although her early retirement goal wasn't specific, she went about exploring creative outlets and experiences. She signed up for dance classes, auditioned for a docent position at an art and design museum (and became the head of the docent corps for two years), and expressed herself daily by curating and wearing unique fashion choices.

One day a man stopped her on a New York City street to ask if he could photograph her. She hesitated at first but ultimately agreed. Although she didn't know anything about Instagram, she learned how to best use its capabilities, posting his photos of her in various fashion statements and adding lots of relevant hashtags. Now she is an Instagram fashion influencer (@Artfulcitystyle) with more than forty thousand followers. She acts in TV commercials, models in runway shows, and is interviewed in fashion magazines worldwide—all in "retirement" at the age of fifty-plus. Her *goal* wasn't specific, but it was clear enough to guide her to her creative passions. There was a *gap* in fashion icons for women fifty and older, and there are *gains* for the women she inspires daily, for the designers whose creations she models, and for her own fun in her second act.

Think Small

If you want to be a game designer, start by creating one concept for one game. If you want to be an inventor, start with one invention. Why start modestly? Putting too much pressure on yourself might backfire, whereas the act of conceiving one game has just enough stress to excite you and is a finite goal, which is likely achievable. If you set too big a goal, you might hamstring yourself. Setting more than one goal at a time can be daunting. One goal is all it takes to move toward determining a gap.

Of course, grand goals are divine. World peace. No poverty. And many other noble pursuits. However, thinking too big can make a goal seem indefinable or unmanageable. For instance, during a drought many public service ads ask people to save water. That's good general advice. It might be more helpful if they were to ask people to set smaller, more practical goals or objectives, such as "Take a shorter shower," "Wash your car by hand," or "Don't flush after number one." (Sorry.)

Thinking smaller doesn't mean the goal is not worthwhile. My daughter was taking a summer course at Harvard about writing short stories. When she called home, I would ask about the day's lesson. Up until then, I had written only nonfiction, plus one screenplay when I was in graduate school. An educational opportunity presented itself; I was learning how to write a short story, gleaning information from my daughter. My goal: As a creative break at lunchtime, I would try to write one short story. And I'd keep at it until it worked. One. Short. Story. At. Lunch. Since then, literary journals have published my short stories, and two stories have been nominated for awards. But I started small when the opportunity presented itself.

Don't worry about your ego when setting a goal. As the Cubist writers might have written: a goal is a goal is a goal. Smaller goals are often more manageable.

Be Flexible

If your goal is to create visual art, that's great. You have a set goal. If your journey seeking inspiration for your art takes you in another promising direction—say it inspires song lyrics—perhaps you can reset your goal. Some creative professionals practice more than one art form—for instance, someone might be a visual artist as well as a songwriter. Go with it. Lean in to pivoting when it's beneficial.

Your goal might start out in one direction, and your thinking or journey might lead you to another goal. Be open to how things progress. Think back to the creation of Instagram (which started out as a location-based app) or to Lin-Manuel Miranda, who set out to write the first song for a mixtape before finally ending up with the goal of writing a stage musical.

The Three Gs are fluid!

If you set a goal, think of ways that will help you to stick to it. Make a commitment. Your present self might get frustrated along the way, but think of how happy you'll make your future self if you keep at it. You'll read more about emotional obstacles in chapter 7.

Think about Responding to a Need

Let's say you need to solve a problem for your own company or your employer wants you to solve a problem or address a need. Or a family member or friend might ask you for an idea.

If your employer wants to increase sales, manufacture a more accessible product, or streamline a service, you're facing a fairly set goal. I say "fairly" because the goal your company is setting might not be on target. It's only after investigation or research that you may realize it's the wrong goal or a goal that needs to be modified. Ask probing questions to ascertain if the goal is the correct one.

Alternatively, let's say you want to solve a problem, with no external request. You might have a special or strong need or passion to explore. You've heard "Necessity is the mother of invention"—in other words, when a need arises, you must find a new way to do something or create something. For example, Kelu Yu, a doctoral student in the Department of Materials Science and Engineering at National University of Singapore, was inspired to find a new way for her father, who had glaucoma, to examine his eyes at home.

Glaucoma is an eye condition affecting approximately 64 million people and requires frequent eye exams at the doctor's office or hospital. Yu explains, "My father was diagnosed with glaucoma in 2019 and suffered from constant eye pain and headache. This personal experience motivated me to delve deeper into the disease and treatments.... The field of glaucoma has lagged far behind in developing a safe, accurate, low cost, at-home eye pressure sensor."[11]

With Si Li and David Lee, Kelu Yu created HOPES (Home Eye Pressure E-Skin Sensor), a wearable biomedical device for pain-free, low-cost, at-home intraocular pressure (IOP) testing. Powered by patent-pending sensor technology and artificial intelligence, HOPES is a convenient platform for users to monitor their own IOP.[12]

Crises give rise to urgent needs: war, famine, pandemic, tsunami, and other acts of nature often prompt architects, scientists, physicians, biotech companies, and industrial designers to rethink or set new immediate goals.

Ways of Finding Goals

I would bet Sal Khan was content at his hedge fund job when he began remotely tutoring his cousin, Nadia, who was struggling with unit conversion in her math class. "This 'Swiss-cheese' *gap* [my emphasis] in her knowledge was not allowing her to be placed in the more advanced math track," states the Khan Academy website.[13] Nadia's improved math skills and the interest and demand by other family members for Khan's math tutorials led Khan to a career goal he had not anticipated. Khan's is a wonderful story of how a goal presents itself when you see a worthwhile gap or gap + gain, even a "Swiss-cheese" gap. But it's just one of many ways to find your goal. Here is a roundup of discussed techniques and more:

- *Notice a gap.* Or a gain, a research finding, a situation, or a gap + a gain presents itself (as it did for Khan), and you grab an opportunity.

- *See what pops into your head.* In a single moment, you're conscious of the spark or seed of a goal, when you realize what could be an idea.

- *Challenge the status quo.* Employ unconventional thinking. Go against prevailing conventions.

- *Follow a passion.* Form a goal out of love for a subject, activity, or a combo of things.

- *Give a goal time to take shape.* You further explore a subject or options to guide the goal. Allow enough time for your goal to hatch.

- *Be open to serendipity.* You stumble onto a goal through observation, curiosity, or conversation.

- *Improvise until you find it.* You explore a general direction and figure out a goal on that journey. You discover it.

- *Change course.* After looking at data or thinking about a goal, you realize it might not be the right time for this goal and you pivot or look for a different goal to emerge.

- *Consider not telling others about your goal.* This seems counterintuitive, but not confiding in others can help you maintain focus, avoid the doubt associated with naysaying, and keep the "that won't work" comments at bay to free you to ideate.

- *Push past your first goal.* Part of the process is to always ask yourself, "What else have you got?" Can you push your thinking past your first thought? In retrospect, your first thought might be fantastic. That happens. Best practice, however, says to push past it to find an idea that's truly worthwhile.

- *Push better.* Determine the gap and gain. Bring on the passion.

UNLOCK YOUR CREATIVE POTENTIAL

After completing this chapter, here are your action steps:

Think about how the Three Gs can help you unlock an idea, crystallize an idea, or amplify your idea. Answer these questions to get going:

- If you're excited about doing something, do you see an urgent need or a desire for it?

- Have you challenged the status quo? (Should you?) What would be disruptive to current systems?

- What would be the wrong goals to pursue?

- Where could your passions lead you? To a goal? A gap? A gain?

BUILD A CREATIVE HABIT

Ask "What if...?" Asking what-if questions pushes you to imagine or create. They invite you to speculate beyond your own experience, to wonder what something might be like if...

And it's a helpful tool for forming a goal if you don't have one at the start. You'll recall the example in chapter 2, when Moty Avisar and Alon Geri, Israeli fighter pilots and cofounders of Surgical Theater, asked themselves, "What if surgeons could train like fighter pilots, previewing their surgical procedures like fighter pilots pre-flying their mission?"

My second-favorite prompt is "If only…" This phrase gives you the freedom to talk about something you want to happen or be true. If only I could record my thoughts without writing or speaking. If only there were digital twins, second selves of people, who could survive with people's ideas and knowledge intact forever.

The value of these types of questions or prompts is that you're speculating on a possibility beyond your own experience.

CHAPTER 4

GAP

Everyone complains that it has all been done before,
but we haven't even begun. There's an incredible
amount of new tricks up good people's sleeves.
TIBOR KALMAN, GRAPHIC DESIGNER

If you are feeling cramped by business opportunities here on Earth, have you considered the potential gains from businesses providing services for people and companies working in outer space?

The founders of a California start-up called Inversion have the *goal* of changing what outer space is used for, to expand what we could think of as the space economy. The *gain?* "You could do these cool things—whether it be asteroid mining or lunar sample return or research or manufacturing in space—but you also have to do the return," cofounder and chief executive Justin Fiaschetti said.[1] Inversion's cofounders saw a big, new *gap*: returnable rockets and vehicles to transport valuable cargo from outer space back to Earth.

What's a Gap?

A *gap* is a missing piece that fills a need—an area not yet explored or underexplored, a question not yet asked, or a population not addressed or underserved. A gap can occur in any discipline; in any form; for any population or population sample of any size, type, or location; for any system, in any situation, in any location, and for any conditions (such as weather, extreme heat or cold). Whether your goal is to design a new device or structure, write a story, create a digital game aimed at seniors (a definite gap), sell more product, open a restaurant, build a crowd-sourced furniture delivery app, build a better whatsit, determine if your goal will fill a *gap*.

Here's a mind-blowing example. The official mission of the James Webb Space Telescope—a collaborative effort by the U.S. National Aeronautics and Space Administration (NASA), the Canadian Space Agency, and the European Space Agency—is to explore a realm of cosmic history that was inaccessible to Hubble and every telescope before it. In an article in the *New York Times*, Wendy Freedman of the Department of Astronomy and Astrophysics at the University of Chicago is quoted discussing the James Webb Space Telescope's capabilities: "Today we have a chance to learn something about the early universe....As we have gotten increasingly higher accuracy, the issue has changed—we can now ask if there are cracks in our current standard cosmological model. Is there some *new missing* [my emphasis] fundamental physics?"[2]

In the same article, Klaus Pontoppidan, an astronomer with the Space Telescope Science Institute, said, "The telescope was built to answer questions we didn't know we had."[3]

Every unique and worthwhile idea must address a gap—some knowledge, information, entertainment, utility, method, system, framework, creative work, and so on that is missing in any discipline. There is almost always something that remains to be done or learned in any field. If you're not filling a gap, then you're likely not contributing something worthwhile, interesting, inspiring, challenging, original (entirely new), or creative (a twist on an existing idea, not entirely original). There are always gaps in knowledge. You might be thinking, *How would I find a gap?* Think:

- What is needed? A product, system, device, art form, artistic interpretation, business, entertainment, transportation, leadership method, or something else?

- In any field, what is the key question that remains to be solved or answered?

- Think about an audience. This could be a demographic, a psychographic (in marketing, a way of classifying people according to their attitudes, decision-making style, or interests), or really any audience.

- What has been underfunded or underresearched? For example, neglected tropical diseases or science for the most neglected patient populations are typically underfunded.

- What has not yet been interpreted or made clear? What would move the discipline forward?

- What has not yet solved the issues of homelessness, world hunger, clean water for all, extreme weather, sustainability, affordable housing, or curbing carbon emissions? For example, the Danish toy company LEGO promised to start making all LEGO bricks from sustainable sources, recently unveiling its prototype for a recycled PET brick that is nearly identical to the usual brick.[4]

Many gaps have a direct relationship to a lack of equity. There are plenty of problems to solve and gaps to fill. Plenty.

If you have knowledge of something useful in your field, think about how it could be useful in a different field or different region. Do you know of something useful that could be adapted to another field—for example, an aviation-style checklist to help hospitals prevent errors in procedures, or a pilot-type simulation training tool that can be used to train surgeons. Here are more questions to consider. Is there...

- a missing piece in research or a product/service category? A void?

- a crack in the research?

- an area that has not been explored at all? (For example, until recently, the thought of regularly transporting cargo from outer space back to Earth might have seemed unattainable.)

- an underserved or unconsidered group of people?

- a lack of understanding about how something works?

- a method that should be tested or retested?

- a new method of delivery not used?

- a new class of drugs or a new operating system? (For example, using mRNA science to create medicine is a fundamentally different approach from what had been done for years.)

- a multidisciplinary platform approach?

- a plant, process, or system not yet examined?

- a more sustainable method?

- a toxic-free production method?

- a child-safe method?

- a way to address the world's endemic crises (hunger, poverty, human trafficking, and so on)?

- something in your field that can be merged with a system in another field to create a new consequential system?

Think about access, for instance, and literally filling a gap. Who doesn't have access to important things, information, education, or water? In partnership with the agency Media.Monks, Reporters Without Borders, an international organization that advocates for press freedom worldwide, had a *goal*: they wanted young people living under censorship to have access to information. The game Minecraft offered a way to fill this *gap* in access to information— this highly successful game is accessible to millions and became a loophole to bypass censorship. Censored articles by acclaimed journalists were republished as uncensored Minecraft books within the game. The Uncensored Library reached over 20 million gamers, was mentioned in more than 790 news articles, and became an educational tool in schools and universities. The library will stay open, giving the right to access information back to young people.[5]

A *gap* could be any number of things—a type, a size, a location, a category, an analysis, a system, a product, and so on. You never know what will click. Who would have imagined people could book commercial flights on rockets into outer space during the early twenty-first century or remove carbon dioxide from the air with a carbon removal factory?

If your goal is to get people to comply with a doctor's or nurse's orders, to feel less uneasy in a medical setting, or to speed recovery in patients, the gap might be related to something that is *not* addressing how people feel. Enter Robin the Robot. Literally. Robin, from Expper Technologies, is an artificial intelligence–based robot companion designed to aid with several issues among children in hospitals and dental offices, such as easing anxiety and reducing stress. "The goal was to create a technology that's not just a device—but a peer and friend," says entrepreneur Karen Khachikyan, CEO and founder of Expper Technologies.[6]

Robin the Robot offers multiple first-of-its-kind gains and fills several gaps. She can recognize children's emotions and act like a friend, she is an assistant to the medical personnel, and she acts to reduce fear and stress in children, fostering cooperation with the medical staff.[7]

Let's look at Expper Technologies' Robin the Robot through the lens of the Three Gs. The *goal* is to get children to comply with a doctor's or nurse's order, to feel more comfortable, and to be less stressed in a medical setting. The *gap*? Nothing existed to manage these issues other than parents, guardians, or the medical staff themselves. The *gain*? Robin reduces children's fears, lowers their stress, and fosters cooperation.

Seeing a similar gap, my university students and I set a low-tech goal of creating a coloring book based on animal similes for children who are hospitalized, to help them describe their physical or emotional pain, which is often difficult for children. Does your head feel like a bear is sitting on it? Does your belly ache as if a kangaroo punched it? My university students illustrated those imaginary scenarios that the children could select to color.

Once you realize a gap, explore whether your solution might be multi-platform. For example, Eitan Grinspun, former chair of the Columbia University Computer Science grad school, says, "Our insights are applicable to a wide range of problems that involve anticipating the movement of flexible, stretchable structures."[8] Perhaps you've solved one problem, then realize your solution is applicable elsewhere. We call this multi-application thinking. Grinspun and his team did just that. Grinspun's research in discrete differential geometry has been instrumental in animated films, including Disney's *Tangled* and *Moana*. His former Columbia University team also explored applications of its research in medicine, robotics, electronics, and infrastructure. For example, Grinspun and his students helped civil engineers at MIT develop a new method for deploying underwater Internet cables that will prevent them from becoming tangled on their way down to the ocean floor.

A gap might not be entirely novel—it could be your unique spin, treatment, or investigation, significant or small. You'd think New York City would have been home to every possible cuisine, given the diversity of the city's population and its international visitors and citizens. Chef David Chang's command of the "humble ramen noodle" and his different approach to food changed the culinary landscape of New York and eventually the world.

SPOTLIGHT   CHEF DAVID CHANG / MOMOFUKU

Many American college students sustain themselves on instant ramen noodles in a cup, an inexpensive fast meal. In 2004, when David Chang opened Momofuku Noodle Bar, a small restaurant in Manhattan's East Village serving ramen noodles, he changed New Yorkers' minds about the dish.

Chang's use of Asian flavors and fresh ingredients is part of a new food movement that helped change notions about Asian food. Influenced by his time living in Japan, dining in ramen shops, and talking with their chefs, as well as his formal training at the French Culinary Institute and his work as a cook at Craft restaurant in Manhattan, Chang found his *goal.* Chang's obsession with ramen noodles drove him to try every possible recipe. A lot of creative professionals think this way. It's about seeking a solution everywhere until you find one.

Momofuku means "lucky peach" in Japanese. Chang chose the name for this first restaurant as an homage to Momofuku Ando, the inventor of instant ramen, the food that gets students, Chang included, through college dorm life.

The *gap* Chang filled is clear to everyone now. Chang's different approach to what most of the world considers inexpensive dishes, ramen noodles and pork buns, redefined Asian cuisine.

Many say Chang is the defining chef of our times. Besides his restaurants, his Netflix series, *Ugly Delicious*, also filled a *gap*. Although heavily influenced by Anthony Bourdain's thinking and show, Chang's program probes more deeply into the sociocultural roots of food. Unlike TV food competitions, recipe programs, or travel and food programming, Chang's unyielding passion and curiosity leads him to delve deeply. "Watching him deconstruct, say, the roots of fried chicken across cultures 'makes us more curious eaters and more curious people in the world,'" pastry chef Christina Tosi told the *Washington Post.* "It's not food for entertainment, it's not for [the] wow factor. It's to feed you in a different way."[9]

Consider Newly Available Technologies

Sometimes a goal and a gap must be in sync with the times; they might be dependent upon available technology. Conversely, they can spur technology. Surprisingly, the first can opener wasn't invented until almost fifty years after the invention of the can. As you might surmise, the invention of the can, an intriguing story that started with Napoleon Bonaparte, was about food preservation. In 1795 Napoleon offered a prize to anyone who could invent a way to preserve food so it wouldn't spoil during his army's long journeys. The winner devised glass jars with lids. The world's first can of iron and tin was made by Peter Durand, a British inventor who was awarded a patent by King George III in 1810. To open these cans, however, people had to use a knife or hammer and chisel, which led to the loss of many a finger. As cans started to penetrate the regular market, the idea of a dedicated can opener emerged.

Ezra J. Warner, a North American, patented the first can opener on January 5, 1858.[10]

When affordable 3D printers came on the market, creators and makers were thrilled to have this new tech at their fingertips. What if your goal were to solve the endemic crisis of homelessness using a 3D printer? Such a home undoubtedly would fill a gap. Recent housing enterprises prove 3D printing technology is a viable way to quickly build affordable housing.

3D printing is an additive manufacturing method, which uses machines to deposit thin layers of plastic, metal, concrete, proprietary concrete materials, and other materials atop one another, building a three-dimensional object. 3D printers are used across industries to create various objects, from art to prosthetics. With a goal of providing "housing first" to end chronic homelessness, a company named ICON filled a *gap* by using 3D printing to build permanent housing for people who are experiencing homelessness.

3D printing brings affordability to the construction industry in a confluence of economic, demographic, and technological developments. This technology, faster and cheaper than conventional construction, could help address out-of-reach home prices for many would-be home buyers as well as homelessness for thousands—those affected by long-term homelessness as well as by evictions and job loss. This confluence supports the *goal*, illuminates the *gap*, and yields a worthwhile *gain*.

To pinpoint a *gap*, such as the one in housing construction, train yourself to look for an insight—a human truth. Conducting research is a given for scientists, social scientists, and many other experts, whether in a lab, in a studio, or out in the field, which may be in the built or natural environment.

If you're not a scientist, you can gather information related to your goal by conducting casual or anecdotal research with an eye toward discovering an insight. Stay open to any enlightening bit of information that points to a solution you hadn't anticipated. I can't overstate the importance of finding an insight into a behavior that leads to noticing a gap. Think of contemporary technology, products, services, and brands that have come to market and are doing well—3D printers, dating apps, drones, rideshare, ingredient-and-recipe meal kits, virtual reality universes, Alodia, Bombas, Girlfriend Collective, Kiswe, Material Kitchen, Peleton, and UNTUCKit—and reverse engineer their ideas using the Three Gs to see what gaps they filled.

Do Your Research

If your goal is company-driven, your company or an external research firm might supply an insight. Sometimes that research is thorough, and other times it's skimpy. If you're working on your own or need supplementary information, conduct a literature search—a systematic, thorough search of all types of existing work on your topic, such as books, articles, and peer-reviewed articles. Search engines, databases, and online libraries make this easily doable.

Plan your search by finding the right keywords and phrases. You can check:

- dictionaries and thesauri—general or subject-specific, online or printed.
- keywords and descriptors used in key journal articles.
- subject headings, phrase lists, or other lists of controlled vocabulary in individual databases.

Phrase searching helps refine your search by allowing you to look for words together in a phrase, in the order specified—typically by surrounding the words with quotation marks. Most databases support this type of search. Google Scholar is also a great resource. If you're seeking public opinion about a topic, search social media with hashtag words or phrases. Conduct social listening on social media platforms—read what a cross-section of people are saying to get a consensus.

Once you gather information and analyze your data, seek an insight that points to a gap and eventually to a gain, in order to form a goal resulting in an idea that is beneficial.

Data is a great resource that informs potential gaps. For example, data might show that people who tend not to make purchases on their mobile phones may do so for reasons that have nothing to do with the online brand experience. If you examine this data closely, you may learn that they have payment security concerns or do not trust the site; their decision was not about the online mobile shopping experience or a preference for the desktop experience. Therefore, the data would inform the gap—if you're about to open a shop that offers a mobile experience, make sure consumers know that the payment portal is secure.

You might notice a pattern—a data pattern, something people do over and over, or something that recurs in nature that might solve a problem or that needs to be addressed.

Mindfully observing people and conducting social listening— causal research—are much less scientific approaches but nonetheless have great potential. For example, you notice that many people prefer to exercise at home, so you invent a compact yet high-performance home workout system. Or you notice people don't enjoy being tethered to their phones by corded headphones, so you invent wireless earbuds.

Like observational comedians, you might be good at recognizing a phenomenon in the environment or in people's behaviors. You can recognize a characteristic of human behavior because you're observant and always seeking to understand human behavior. A prepared mind recognizes this kind of phenomenon. Tip: Listen to observational comedians' acts or read their writing.

Notice Possibilities around You

Another way to find a gap is to stay open to possibilities. If you're only in the realm of "Well, we've-always-done-it-this-way," you may never find a gap. Stay open to possibilities—see potential everywhere and in everything. It's a wonderful way to view the world! Seeing potential in everything and everyone is a golden habit to build.

You can notice things serendipitously. Maybe you were seeking an answer to one question when a different answer presented itself. For example, Viagra's active ingredient, sildenafil, was being tested to treat a heart ailment. 3M's Post-it Notes were invented when Spencer Silver was studying adhesives in his lab; eventually he and a colleague, Art Fry, realized a use for this low-tack adhesive. Charles Goodyear invented vulcanized rubber by accident. These were all serendipitous findings that came out of other experiments.

Inventors or tinkerers might note a gap while they're tinkering, taking things apart, building hybrids, and so on. For example, you may take a radio apart to see how it functions, which leads to an original thought about an alternative way to transmit sound or to use a lighter material to create a more portable unit.

Start Making or Doing

Many artists, writers, composers, and choreographers create by doing. They start writing, choreographing, or painting and allow the creative process to lead them to an idea. Inventors or aspiring inventors might assemble, tinker, or take things apart to see how they work.

Director Henri-Georges Clouzot and cinematographer Claude Renoir made a documentary film, *The Mystery of Picasso*. As we watch Picasso paint, we realize his process is spontaneous—each form he paints brings him to another; nothing is preconceived. His free-form association continues. Five hours later, Picasso declares that he will have to discard the canvas: "Now that I begin to see where I'm going with it, I'll take a new canvas and start again." Picasso used the process of painting to find inspiration and direction while painting; he didn't plan before he began painting.

Similarly, many renowned writers say they don't plan—they allow the creative process of writing to take over as they go. For example, Stephen King said he doesn't outline his stories.[11]

Of course, other writers do plan, but that doesn't prevent the writing process from presenting itself along the way. John Irving says, "I always begin with a last sentence; then I work my way backwards, through the plot, to where the story should begin."[12] He says he needs to know what type of story he is writing—exuberant, mournful—and what type of language describes the end of the story. Important connections are known to him, and Irving needs to know what's waiting for him at the end. However, Irving allows his creative process to blossom as he goes, which makes the journey worthwhile.

Author Alan Hollinghurst says his books creep up on him slowly. Things come at him from different directions, and they accumulate. He doesn't start until he knows the entire architecture. He has a clear plan: episodes, revelations, phrases. But quite a lot is still unknown, so the writing is an exciting process with discoveries along the way.[13]

Engage with Other People

I haven't mentioned the benefits of discussing pain points, subjects, or behaviors with other people. Dialogue with others, especially with a diverse group of people that gives you different and multiple perspectives, could spark recognition of a goal or a gap. Too often particular groups of people are excluded from discussions about ideas. Some mainstream brands, for example, do not invest in inclusive design.

Note that you don't *need* to mention your goal to others. Counsel from potential naysayers isn't productive unless they are experts in the field. Even then, many people succeed going against the old guard.

Nonetheless, the practice of exchanging ideas has an illustrious history. The café culture of early twentieth-century Paris fostered intellectual and artistic discussions among innovative artists, writers, and philosophers about issues, literature, politics, society, art, and more. "Due to café culture, Montparnasse became the artistic hub of the world during the interwar period. From Picasso to Hemingway, the place to be for these revolutionary thinkers was the Café de la Rotonde. Here in this corner of Paris, ideas on life and death were transformed."[14]

Let Your Subconscious Work on the Gap

Mind wandering, in contrast to tightly focused cognition, is a kind of spacing out, thinking without focusing. Writers and artists are good at allowing their minds to wander, incubating their thoughts, and allowing for connections to develop or crystallize. By allowing your thinking to incubate, mind wandering might illuminate a gap. It will help unlock your creative potential.

It's important to allow for an incubation period. A gap might not surface right off; in fact, often you need to allow time for your ideas to hatch, including taking time when you're not consciously thinking about your goal or pinpointing a gap. Coming back to a task after an incubation period usually allows for fresher thinking. Take a break even if it's only twenty minutes to take a walk. Designers often turn to reading literature; seeing films; attending a concert, theater performance, or fine art exhibit; or creating art (drawing, painting, sculpting, or photography). Some designers prefer semiconscious behaviors—like doodling or folding paper into shapes—which allow for productive mind wandering. Psychologists say such activity might be especially productive if the mind is turning over a problem.[15] When your brain is not consciously directing your thoughts and your mind is freely wandering—say, on a walk—alpha brain waves, which are associated with imaginative, creative thought, might occur.

Zachary Irving, professor at the University of Virginia's Corcoran Department of Philosophy, researches mind wandering. "We find a pattern that is really similar to what you find in creative thinking tasks," Irving said. "That became a central part of our hypothesis, that mind-wandering is this meandering thought that is similar to the thought processes that underlie creative thinking. It fits intuitively, and now we had neural evidence to support that picture."[16]

When I am exercising or dancing, I am best able to synthesize the research I've gathered or see a problem in a new light. Or take my friend, Jack, who was sitting on a park bench, no book or phone in hand. Jack's friend walked by and asked, "What are you doing?"

"Working," Jack replied.

Jack wasn't being flip—he was working. Rather than directing his attention to the problem at hand at his desk, Jack was sitting on a bench watching people and dogs pass by—letting his mind wander on purpose. Although he seemed to be doing nothing, Jack was employing unguided attention, allowing his mind to move from topic to topic, to explore without an intentional focus on the business problem he needed to solve.

Undoubtedly, you find yourself working and then your mind wanders—perhaps to a love interest or dream scheme. You could use this common state of consciousness to help you think creatively or imaginatively—to allow your brain to explore. When your mind is wandering, be sure not to ruminate or fixate on an issue or situation. Rather, allow for exploratory daydreaming.

Why does the mind wander?

"One hypothesis I like is that mind-wandering serves the purpose of exploration," explains Irving. "Without knowing it, you are generating creative ideas, or broadly exploring a base of ideas."[17]

However you choose to incubate—with semiconscious behaviors, mind wandering, changing activities, taking a break, seeking a new perspective—stepping back to expand your understanding is best practice to unlock your creative potential.

Finding an Insight

Let's recap some ways you can use to find an insight:

- *Find the pain points.* The difficulties people experience with a product, service, or sector might lead to innovation or creative ideas.

- *Challenge the status quo.* Create alternatives, work-around solutions, or new ways of doing something. Streaming music, for instance, is an alternative to buying music embedded on hard objects.

- *Look for incongruities.* Find the things, data, trends, or behaviors that are inconsistent with how most businesses or disciplines operate.

- *Use analogies.* Co-opt methods, systems, intelligence, or paths employed in other disciplines. For example, TikTok relies on artificial intelligence for its algorithms for users' "For You" pages.

- *Do or make.* Writing or making something is one way to experiment with articulating an idea. Writing or making—doing—becomes a process of discovery. When you search for an insight through the process of making or doing rather than immediately jumping on a vague idea, you're likely to get better results.

- *Ask yourself imagination-building questions.* What if I were to…? What if I swapped out…? What if I reverse this? What if I change the shape?

- *Think about intersections of factors.* Such factors could include technology, demographics, trends, the economy, and social movements. For example, think about 3D printed housing, which came about through a confluence of tech, demographic, and social factors.

- *Conduct real-world observations.* Go on site to see how people behave. Visit a supermarket, for example, to see how people select consumer packaged goods.

Remember that you must prepare your mind for finding an insight. Practice mindful observation, be curious, and see potential in all.

UNLOCK YOUR CREATIVE POTENTIAL

After completing this chapter, here are your action steps:

Think about a gap you've noticed or researched, or something you'd like to see in the world that you think doesn't exist yet. Would your potential idea be filling a gap or taking advantage of an opportunity? Is it worth it? How do you know that?

Use the Three Gs—the keys to unlock your creativity:

Do you have a goal in mind?

Have you noticed or researched a gap in a field or discipline?

Would your idea offer a benefit—a gain to individuals, society, creatures, or our planet? Might it move the discipline or society forward?

More specifically related to this chapter:

Do you think you could use data to pinpoint a gap?

In what way could challenging the status quo in your industry or area of interest possibly lead to recognition of a gap?

Have you tried mind wandering to allow your creative thinking to incubate?

BUILD A CREATIVE HABIT

Allow time for incubation. Don't rush creative thinking or ideation. My best ideas come after I've let them incubate for a minimum of twenty-four hours. If I have the luxury of time, my ideas really come together after weeks of incubation.

After you've considered your goal, gap, and gain, let the Three Gs incubate—allow your subconscious mind to do some work. When you're daydreaming, showering, or walking, your mind is still working on your idea—*if you've done the preliminary work*. Take a bit of time away from directly focusing on forming your idea. Feed your thinking, too. Read great literature. See a well-crafted film. Go to a museum. Read about a scientific discovery or a successful business venture. In other words, indulge in whatever nourishes your brain. Then return fresher to focus on your idea.

CHAPTER 5

GAIN

Most entrepreneurial ideas will sound
crazy, stupid and uneconomic, and
then they'll turn out to be right.
REED HASTINGS, CEO, NETFLIX

For a short while, I thought I might want to teach children, or at least that was the career my mother had planned for me. During college I was a student teacher in a sixth-grade classroom in New York City. After that experience I declared grade school teachers to be saints. I quickly abandoned that career path, following my own goal of being a designer and artist. Eventually I did become an educator—in higher education. So it wasn't teaching itself that dissuaded me back then. In fact, I am passionate about teaching my university students.

In that sixth-grade classroom, one boy would hold onto my ankle for the entire class. Another would cry repeatedly. I didn't feel adequately prepared to deal with the vastness of the emotional issues the children brought to the classroom. Unfortunately, there are still far too many children worldwide who face difficulties, or even trauma, stemming from poverty, racism, community or domestic violence, world crises, substance abuse at home, or food insecurity, as well as organic mental or physical disorders or issues that interfere with learning. What I realized in my short time in the sixth-grade classroom is the critical need for good ideas that would help children. Here are two examples of worthwhile ideas.

Disney Pixar's *goal* for its film *Inside Out* was to portray a range of emotions so that children could easily understand their own feelings. The film's message is that emotions are important and need to be recognized and validated. That message filled a critical *gap* in children's film entertainment as well as in the emotional lives of children. The story goes like this: Through the interplay of emotions—Joy, Fear, Anger, Disgust, and Sadness—eleven-year-old Riley, the main character, is striving to achieve emotional balance while navigating a move to a new city, house, and school. The *gain*: helping children identify different emotions to help them better understand what they're feeling. The film also can help parents recognize, accept, and validate their child's emotions.

Samantha Pratt, the CEO and founder of the online platform KlickEngage, had a similar goal—to help all students feel psychologically safe and supported in every environment. KlickEngage achieves this "by amplifying the voices of youth, promoting socioemotional well-being, and increasing the effectiveness of existing interventions through technology."[1] Students who log into KlickEngage for a daily check-in are prompted to "answer 5 simple questions to capture their mood snapshot. It takes fewer than two minutes. Evidence-based color groups help students make sense of the complex emotions. Word associations support expression and connect classrooms through a shared vocabulary. Coping tips help students identify strategies to decompress and release feelings."[2] There are KlickEngage teacher and administrative tools so that teachers and administrators can provide proper support as well as data-driven interventions. There are gains for all involved.

Pratt believes that "unless we address all of the needs of a child and their community, we cannot expect to achieve educational equity."[3]

So, what do the ideas underlying Disney Pixar's film *Inside Out* and KlickEngage have in common? Their *goals* of addressing the emotional needs of children fill a *gap*. The *gain?* Both ideas help children tremendously.

Once you've set a goal and determined whether it fills a gap, assess whether there is a *gain*—a benefit or advantage for people or our planet. Like Samantha Pratt, Kennyjie had a goal of solving an endemic problem. As a twelve-year-old living in Indonesia, Kennyjie contracted dengue fever—a flu-like disease transmitted by mosquitoes. In adulthood, as an industrial designer, Kennyjie noticed that mosquito prevention tactics were inconvenient and ineffective, so he set a *goal* of designing his own. His innovative solution, called Quito, is "a low-cost and sustainable CO_2-based [carbon dioxide–based] mosquito trap designed to reduce mosquito populations, targeted at the context that is most ideal for mosquito-borne diseases transmission—tropical tourism."[4]

What's the *gap* he's filling? Quito produces an artificial human odor that attracts mosquitoes and vacuums them into its chamber. Most devices or sprays are repellents, but Quito attracts and traps mosquitoes, reducing the local mosquito population. The *gain* is reducing the chance of disease transmission in tropical resorts to lessen the possibility of contagion as people travel in and out of the region.

Ideas worth pursuing offer a *gain*—they are worthwhile, useful, or meaningful to people, creatures, or our planet. They inform, entertain, provide a utility, or do something for the greater good.

What's in It for Me?

In one of Bill Watterson's *Calvin and Hobbes* cartoon strips, Calvin, the little boy, answers the phone. The caller asks to speak to Calvin's father. When Calvin responds that his father is not home, the caller asks if Calvin would please take a message. Calvin replies, "What's in it for me?"

How do you determine if the goal and gap produce a gain? Think about what drives people. People respond to ideas, inventions, brands—anything really—because they want what it's offering: a better lifestyle, self-improvement, delicious food, odor-free armpits, a cooler home, more fun, something that helps a toddler sleep on a plane, and so on. People seek a functional or emotional benefit for themselves, their families, their loved ones, their community, the rainforest, or their dog. What's in it for me? For my Uncle Don? The greater community? The world?

During the mid-twentieth century, North American psychologist Abraham Maslow presented his theory of human motivation, proposing five core needs that form the basis for human motivation and therefore influence people's behavior. Maslow arranged the five needs into a pyramid, with physiological needs (such as air, water, food, and sleep) at the bottom, followed by security needs (safety, stability), social needs (love, belonging), ego needs (self-esteem, recognition), and finally, at the pinnacle, self-actualization needs (development, creativity).

Think of our atavistic urges. Beyond our basic need for air, food, and shelter, people want to belong, have friends and family (related to survival and companionship), love interests (related to sex drive and companionship), be stimulated/amused (related to play and gratification), experience things (related to curiosity and participation), and to self-actualize (related to creative growth and intellectual development).

Will the *gain* address one of the following for people?

- Respond to a desire, a wish, or a yearning (think the lottery or Bumble)

- Satisfy a hope with the promise of a positive outcome (think Tonal fitness)

- Address a need, whether emotional or practical, real or imagined (think The Nature Conservancy)

- Point to a need people didn't even realize they had (think Apple's iPhone)

- Solve a problem with the functional benefit of a product or service (think Tylenol)

- Resolve a pain point (think True Name by Mastercard)

- Change perceptions (think Momofuku)

- Provide fun or entertainment as well as a way to connect (think TikTok or Twitch)

- Provide information or education (think Reporters Without Borders' use of Minecraft to get information out to youth under censorship)

- Provide a utility (think Google)

- Advocate (think Southern Poverty Law Center)

- Allow for self-actualization (think online higher education or Alvin Ailey Extension dance classes)

- Provide purpose (think the Peace Corps)

Examples of Gains

An important consideration when coming up with a worthwhile idea is to determine the target audience; it's a crucial factor in advertising, branding, industrial design, interactive design, entertainment programming, copywriting, marketing, and even in teaching.

An idea must have within it some emotional or practical functional benefit for people or someone they care about; otherwise they will not pay attention or will tune out. There's too much going on 24/7.

Inventions

If you were to search the term "great ideas," inventions would undoubtedly pop up. People see inventions as synonymous with ideas. From driverless cars to the James Webb Space Telescope to smartphones, inventions have changed our lives and the world. Inventions may be the one category people think of when they think of idea generation, but they're certainly not the only one.

Not everyone is an inventor. In fact, you might have had an idea for an invention only to realize that you don't have the engineering or technical background to make it happen—that's happened to me many times. That doesn't mean you shouldn't pursue it; people don't always invent alone. Many people collaborate successfully. Or you might have technical expertise but lack business expertise. Not having enough expertise in manufacturing twice prevented me from moving forward on business ideas—I didn't have the know-how or resources to follow it through, but I didn't think to find investors or other experts. Now I'm sorry I didn't.

Many inventions provide a gain by driving progress (depending upon how you look at it), but they also cause harm—pollution, waste, and so on. Today, however, many inventors are thinking sustainably, and that represents important progress too.

The Arts

The gains from the arts include enrichment, enlightenment, insight into humanity and our world, empathy, sharing, and seeing as others see and think. The arts transport us. They transfix. They teach. Each worthwhile novel, short story, poem, song, design, building, sculpture, play, dance, and painting is based on an idea.

In the arts, makers often do not start out by pinpointing their idea, but rather find it along the way, as they work. As pointed out earlier, you can find a gap this way. In an interview in the *Paris Review*, when John Wray asked writer Haruki Murakami about his conscious choices, Murakami replied, "When I start to write, I don't have any plan at all. I just wait for the story to come. I don't choose what kind of story it is or what's going to happen. I just wait. *Norwegian Wood* is a different thing, because I decided to write in a realistic style. But basically, I cannot choose."[5]

Other writers and artists do map things out. If you reverse engineer a great work of art, analyzing it to ascertain the creator's goal, gap, and gain, you'll start to see how the artist thinks. As you can tell from the examples in this book, I deconstruct other people's ideas all the time to learn from them.

Entertainment

Like the arts, the field of entertainment depends upon ideas. Many are formulaic, but others are novel or creative and offer greater gains. If you think about entertainment that has impacted the arts and some that affect society more broadly—from the pioneering public television program *Sesame Street* (entertainment that has enhanced learning in the United States) and millennial favorite *Rick and Morty* to Kathryn Bigelow's *The Hurt Locker* (an arresting look at life in combat in Iraq) or Bong Joon-ho's *Parasite* (a fierce commentary on income inequality)—you start to see the how the creators' goals, gaps, and gains might emerge. I often turn to television programming or films when I need to be transported into an imaginary world.

Education and Information

Ideas fill gaps in knowledge or provide content that enlightens, advises, or educates. In this book I've highlighted the Khan Academy, KlickEngage, Reporters Without Borders, and Tiya Miles's book *All That She Carried: The Journey of Ashley's Sack, a Black Family Keepsake.*

World Issues and Social Good

Ideas can address so many social causes, issues, and endemic problems, as well as aid a great number of people by advancing safety, health, community, education, and the protecting environment. We need ideas to fight droughts and deforestation; afford access to clean water for everyone; prevent, detect, and treat diseases; and develop new medicines.

Products and Services

New products and services emerge all the time. In highly industrialized countries, supermarket and retail shopping outlets are replete with choices. For example, first there was one diet carbonated soft drink, and now there are many. Many companies focus mainly on generating profits. Therefore, if a company's product or service is doing well, other companies try to imitate their success with a very similar offering. When applying the Three Gs, you're focusing on generating worthwhile ideas and are much more likely to think of the triple bottom line—profit, people, and our planet.

Evaluating the Gain

Another way to look at a gain is to determine the *why*: Why do you have this goal? Why is the gap worth filling? Why would people gain from it? As author Simon Sinek says, it's not the *what* or the *how*—it's the underlying *why* that matters.

Kuleana is a 100% plant-based, sushi-grade, ready-to-eat "tuna" made from ingredients including algae, koji (a fungus that grows in East Asia), radish, bamboo, and potato. The team behind Kuleana is passionate about solving an existential environmental sustainability problem. (You might recall I suggested following your passion when setting a goal.) The team designed their alt-tuna, Kuleana, to be prepared as sushi, *nigiri,* carpaccio, poke, or ceviche, which retains the iron, vitamin B12, and omega-3 fatty acids of real tuna without the mercury or the environmental and ethical consequences.

The Kuleana mission statement says, "We start with the why, our why is our vision. Our culture promotes resourceful performance where people come first. We uphold the values of trust, honesty, and passion."[6]

You can evaluate a gain by asking, What's the *why?*

Certainly, plant-based tuna is not for everyone (although I welcome it). That's where knowing your audience comes in. Look at it from other people's point of view. Become the audience, and see it as they see it. Take a survey. Do some research, even if it is casual. Don't assume people's points of view or needs. (See the scenario map and social media research tools—Resource 4—in the resources section at the end of this book.)

Consider whether you're aiming at everyone (almost never a good tactic) or a segment of people. Think about what your audience truly needs or wants. How can you meet the target audience's needs, especially needs unmet by competitors? Does the gain truly add value? Really get to know the group or community your gain serves. What are they doing? What will they be doing next?

Understand the *why* of the audience's behaviors. What are their pain points and barriers? What motivates them? What kind of unsolved problem could your idea solve?

Here's a good example. With so many new natural laundry de-
tergents, moms thought Lysol Laundry Sanitizer, which promised
to kill 99.9% of germs, was too harsh. Lysol found an insight: The
everyday items our kids love the most are actually the germiest.
This led to their marketing idea: Lysol helps you protect what your
child loves most.

This is how Lysol and McCann New York brought the idea to life:
"We celebrated the bond between kids and their stuffed animals—
and helped parents protect it by creating Teddy Repair, a program
designed to disinfect stuffed animals, and even fix those that need
a touch-up after all the love they've been given—all while, crucially,
letting kids track their teddies' journeys." The Teddy Repair sweep-
stakes campaign repaired and sanitized 500 stuffed animals sub-
mitted by parents nationwide. Children could track their plushes
during the repair process, which were fitted with RFID (radio-
frequency identification) bracelets, on their parents' phones.

The result: "We got moms talking, drove sales growth, and
made Lysol relevant to a new category—and teddy caretakers
everywhere."[7]

SPOTLIGHT   *SLAVE PLAY* BY JEREMY O. HARRIS

Slave Play is a play that "imagines a radical form of role-playing
for sexually frustrated interracial couples as a way of exploring the
lingering effects of slavery in America."[8]

In an interview with Tonya Pinkins for the *American Theater*,
the playwright Jeremy O. Harris explained his thinking and goal.
When he was at a party with friends, a "liberal" man was talking
about enjoying rough sex with a woman who demanded it that way.
Harris found it odd that everyone was casually discussing this and
went on to engage in a dialogue with the man. Harris asked the
man if he identified as a male feminist; the man said, "Yes."

Harris responded, "'Great. Now if she was Black, would you feel as comfortable telling all of us about this in this way?' And the entire energy in the room changed immediately…" The conversation continued, piquing Harris' interest in its provocations.

Pinkins' question elicited an exclusive interview response from Harris about his goal as a playwright. "…Because there was only one other person of color in this conversation, and we were laughing at the discomfort that all the white people had at what for us was a very casual question. I was like: This is theatre. This is what theatre should do: Untangle responses like this. So that started it."[9]

The *gap*? There are few produced Black playwrights, and Harris is the only one tackling the legacy of slavery in terms of interracial sexual dynamics and master-slave sexual scenarios.

The *gain* is significant. *Slave Play* breaks taboos, ignites conversations, and creates a brave space. Harris is writing a screenplay with producer Bruce Cohen, who said of *Slave Play*, "The play is exploring so many things that are on people's minds right now in this really complicated, difficult time. A lot of it's about race, but not just about race—about gender, about identity, about expression, about how people connect and interact or aren't allowed to."[10]

Slave Play is the recipient of the Rosa Parks Playwriting Award, the Lorraine Hansberry Playwriting Award, the Lotos Foundation Prize in the Arts and Sciences, and the 2018 Paula Vogel Award.

🏆 UNLOCK YOUR CREATIVE POTENTIAL 🏆

After completing this chapter, here are your action steps:

Think about a gain you'd like to see in the world. Worthwhile ideas contribute not only to business success and the economy but to social well-being, ecological concerns, to the health and safety of communities, the advancement of disciplines and knowledge, to the arts, and to the interests of individuals. Answering these questions will set you on the path toward assessing the gain:

- Is the benefit worth the cost of developing the idea?
- Does the gain align with people's aspirations, desires, or needs, and with society's?
- Does the gain do any harm? For this idea to happen, does any community have to lose?
- Is there an insight you can point to?

BUILD A CREATIVE HABIT

Ask penetrating, disarming, transgressive, or challenging questions. Keep asking questions until you get to the crux of the matter. Even ask provocative questions, as did Jeremy O. Harris.

Dig deep. Then deeper. But if you don't find what you're looking for in one hole, move over and dig a new hole.

NOTES: YOUR IDEAS

What is one of your goals that would really propel your company, career, discipline, or life forward?

_____

_____

_____

_____

_____

Are you aware of a gap in that discipline, field, industry, or sector that aligns with your goal?

_____

_____

_____

_____

Who or what would gain if you were to achieve your goal?

_____

_____

_____

_____

CHAPTER 6

DIVERSITY, EQUITY, AND INCLUSION

Amplifying the Three Gs

The need for innovation to grow, compete, and
transform has never been greater—and we believe
diversity is essential to driving this innovation.
JULIE SWEET, CEO, ACCENTURE NORTH AMERICA

DEI is the X factor. By inviting multiple perspectives, diversity, equity, and inclusion reveal the vantage points of a wide range of people. Those diverse perspectives, which will undoubtedly be different from yours, will allow you to view your idea differently, anew. Your idea can be dramatically improved by thinking about it in a new way.

Taking multiple perspectives—that is, looking at a goal, a gap, a gain, a partially realized idea, or a fully fledged idea from viewpoints different from your own—helps you perceive multiple scenarios, multiple gaps, and potentially multiple gains, ultimately resulting in better ideas that appeal to more people in more meaningful ways.

We each have our own perspective, our own view of the world shaped by our experiences, our communities, families, and education. This personal perspective is the lens through which we see the world and ourselves in it. Multiple perspective taking allows you to mentally walk in others' shoes, to look at a situation, an idea, a life lived, or an event from the viewpoints of people who are different from you, who have had different experiences. That shift in perspective adds a fuller dimension to the Three Gs.

By considering things you didn't think to consider before, you will assuredly find ideas of greater value to individuals, culture, and society. Fresh perspectives also lead to additional questions. By asking more questions of diverse people, you keep widening your scope and the impact of your idea. Here are three questions to ask: What goal can I set to have the best possible gain for the most possible people? Is there a gap I hadn't considered before I took multiple perspectives? Is there a gain that is more equitable?

DEI also combats groupthink—that is, the conformity that happens when similar people, who might be unfamiliar with outside perspectives, work in a group. A team or a community of similar people tend to think similarly and might not bring anything dissenting or challenging to a discussion. If you view the Three Gs from other perspectives, you will begin to see how age, gender identity, neurodivergence, culture, race, ethnicity, religion, or community characteristics might affect and ultimately amplify your concept. Not only will you get unfamiliar perspectives from a diverse group, but you likely will get different problem-solving input as well. When you augment the Three Gs with DEI, you will find valuable insights into other people that will lead you to more ideas, better ideas, more *significant* ideas.

In the introduction, I told you about Matt Hite, Ken Jones, and other devoted people who brought the Microsoft Xbox Adaptive Controller to market. Microsoft's project teams took multiple perspectives. They partnered with experts—accessibility advocates and gamers with disabilities as well as nonprofit organizations that work with gamers living with disabilities, such as the AbleGamers Charity, the Cerebral Palsy Foundation, SpecialEffect, and Warfighter

Engaged, and many other accessibility community members. DEI amplified this worthwhile idea, turning it into a momentous idea.

Without DEI, you see life through a regular camera lens. DEI presents a way to see life through a wide-angle lens that produces panoramic images to create a more expansive perspective. When you embrace DEI, you put yourself in the path of amplified worthwhile ideas.

Getting Started with DEI

To help my students examine their ideas and subsequent creative solutions, I wrote a social justice treatise. Answering the following questions, which are extracted from that treatise, will not only set you on the path to ensuring your idea is responsive to diversity, equity, and inclusion but also make your thinking more consequential. Ask:

- Have I considered how people of different ethnicities may identify with my idea?

- Am I employing a stereotype or trope relative to race, ethnicity, gender identity, sexuality, religion, disability, or age?

- Have I tried swapping the audience for that of another race, ethnicity, gender, age, sexual orientation, or religious group? If so, do any stereotypes emerge?

- Does the idea contribute to any hegemonic systems of oppression?

- Would any group be marginalized by this representation or message? Would any group be demeaned?

- Have I thought about elevating equity?

When you form a goal, try swapping out the audience for that of another country, community, race, ethnicity, religion, gender identity or expression, age, sexual orientation, or religious group or for people living with disabilities to see if it is equitable.

When you fill a gap, is a group or community missing? Are there other groups for whom you could fill gaps? If you expand your sights, all sorts of gaps might become apparent. If you're not looking at the Three Gs from all these different perspectives, you're limiting possible outcomes and potentially fuller ideas.

When you determine a gain, for an idea to win, does someone have to lose? If it's a gain for more communities, then it's a bigger gain. Equity should always be the standard.

If we search for gaps that offer gains to achieve equity, we can form useful goals and generate ideas that are worthwhile. And if we could ensure our ideas improve equity, that would be worthwhile indeed. Ros Atkins did just that. DEI supercharged Atkins's goal. He tackled a thorny gap: the underrepresentation of women in the media—an issue most men in the news media wouldn't touch.

SPOTLIGHT   BBC 50:50 THE EQUALITY PROJECT

After thinking about the issue of equality for a long time, Ros Atkins of the BBC explained, "I became focused on three goals. I wanted: better data on the representation of women in our journalism and content; to explore the impact of embedding representation in our daily editorial and production thinking and processes; and to prove that fair representation is not only a goal to aspire to but one that can be achieved consistently."[1]

To work toward attaining all three *goals*, Atkins and the BBC adopted a new approach to content production and culture change, now known as 50:50. "At the heart of the idea is that if we monitor ourselves, we can generate data for our organizations, while simultaneously influencing our own motivation, awareness and performance. The data would be the engine of change," said Atkins.[2]

The *gap* is the underrepresentation of women in the media worldwide. Just as a lack of ethnic and racial diversity gives an unbalanced picture of society, an underrepresentation of women perpetuates harmful gender stereotypes.

When Atkins first introduced his equity initiative, he faced a lot of questions from colleagues, such as, Is this a quota? His response was that 50:50 is simple, voluntary, and designed to measure the elements of their work that the team themselves control.

Anyone can advance DEI, even if they belong to a dominant group. Atkins is a white man from the BBC news division and not a DEI expert, as Aneeta Rattan, Siri Chilazi, Oriane Georgeac, and Iris Bohnet noted in an article in the *Harvard Business Review*.[3]

What's the *gain?* About creating real cultural change in an organization and the 50:50 project, Nina Goswami, BBC's creative diversity lead, wrote,

> More than 100 organizations across 26 countries have pledged to use the data tool to improve the representation in their content. This change is happening across media, PR and communications, academia, legal and corporate companies.
>
> Finally, we believed that the 50:50 methodology could benefit other areas of representation. To this end, we translated the 50:50 core principles to monitor disability and ethnicity.... We will also support any partners who wish to [implement] 50:50 beyond gender in their organizations. We want to see diverse voices enriching media content across the world.[4]

SPOTLIGHT   **LUIS VON AHN / DUOLINGO**

It's highly likely you've encountered Luis von Ahn's produced ideas. Von Ahn is the inventor of reCAPTCHA and the co-inventor of CAPTCHA. Growing up in Guatemala helped form von Ahn's mission to improve diversity, equity, and inclusion, amplifying his most recent goal—to give everyone access to a private language tutor experience through technology. Von Ahn's is a fascinating case that makes clear why observing a gap, realizing a gain, and setting a goal through the lens of DEI yields an exceptionally worthwhile idea.

When he was in the computer science Ph.D. program at Carnegie Mellon University, von Ahn studied under Manuel Blum, recipient of the 1995 Turing Award. With Blum, von Ahn developed a visual recognition test to prevent bots from spamming websites, a string of squiggly letters that humans can identify but computers can't. They called it the Completely Automated Public Turing Test to Tell Computers and Humans Apart, or CAPTCHA. "We knew it was going to be useful, but there were many uses we hadn't thought of," said von Ahn.[5] Most major websites use CAPTCHA.

In his doctoral thesis, von Ahn introduced the idea of human computation, the concept that laid the groundwork for several of his future innovations, including CAPTCHA (his collaboration with Blum), reCAPTCHA, and Games with a Purpose. With reCAPTCHA, von Ahn's idea was filling a gap and proving its gain. "ReCAPTCHA has facilitated the digitization of about two million books per year from the Google Books project, and more than 13 million articles in the *New York Times* archives dating back to 1851. This has helped make historical works previously confined to specific physical library locations widely available online, opening up possibilities for research and ensuring long-term digital access to a wide range of people," according to the Lemelson-MIT case study website.[6]

After selling reCAPTCHA to Google, von Ahn shifted his goal. He cofounded Duolingo, a platform bringing free and accessible language learning to everyone, helping to remove obstacles to social mobility across the globe. His new *goal* was to "fight socioeconomic disparities by breaking down barriers to education."[7]

Clearly there was a gap and a gain, but why this goal?

When von Ahn was growing up in Guatemala, he saw how poverty bars access to high-quality education. Wealthy families in Guatemala can pay for a quality education, whereas very poor families may not even be able to afford to give their children the opportunity to learn to read and write. A lack of a quality education is a perpetuating factor in inequality in any country. For many in Guatemala, though learning English could offer transformative career opportunities, language instruction is out of reach.

When von Ahn wanted to apply for college in the United States, he had to take an English certification test, but all the seats for the test in Guatemala City were filled. To take the test, he had to fly to El Salvador at a cost of $1,200—clearly an amount many people would not be able to afford. You can see why he, as someone who understood inequality from the inside, formed his goal as he did. DEI amplified his goal.

Von Ahn received the Lemelson-MIT Prize in 2018 for his groundbreaking inventions, commitment to youth mentorship, and dedication to improving the world through technological invention.[8]

And, yes, his worthwhile ideas have come full circle—Duolingo does use the reCAPTCHA he designed.

SPOTLIGHT   ANDREA MOCELLIN / REVOLVE AIR

A goal can't get much grander than "reinventing the wheel." At the Viva Technology Pitch in Paris, Andrea Mocellin said his goal was to do just that. After speaking with Paralympic athletes, Mocellin, a Ferrari designer, viewed his goal through a DEI lens, which supercharged his thinking. The Paralympic athletes told him that if he were to reinvent the wheels of a wheelchair, that would improve their lives. He listened. He realized the gap and the gain. DEI is the X factor once again.

Mocellin reset his *goal* to design a compact wheelchair with modular folding wheels, which would fill an urgent *gap*. For people using wheelchairs, a compact foldable wheelchair would be a huge *gain*.

When wheelchair users fly, they must give up their wheelchairs at the gate. One disability rights activist likens it to watching someone take away her legs. At times, airlines mishandle wheelchairs, leaving them damaged and forcing people to live with broken mobility aids. U.S. senator Tammy Duckworth told *USA Today* that most people do not grasp how damaged or lost wheelchairs adversely affect wheelchair users.[9]

"These medical devices are essentially a part of a disabled person's body," Duckworth said. "Imagine if in a single year (that many) people had their legs broken by an airline as a result of flying. The effect is the same."[10]

Enter Mocellin, whose original goal of reinventing the wheel was grand. He modified his goal: Redesign the wheels on a wheelchair to make the chair more travel-friendly, compact, and portable yet safe and sturdy. When you fold the Revolve Air wheelchair, it takes up 60 percent less space than a standard folding wheelchair. This allows Revolve Air to fit the standard cabin baggage compartment dimensions universally used by airlines. Mocellin's design offers many gains. Users no longer need to check their wheelchairs, where they are at risk from airline handlers, or seek airport assistance. That gives wheelchair users traveling equity and access. The chair also fits easily into a smaller car's trunk, opening up more taxi and travel options.

"With a simple action you can open and close the wheel making it practical and convenient for every user," explains Mocellin. "Its portability is guaranteed with two handles that lock and unlock the wheel when unfolded, giving a second life to the wheel and the demands and constraints of present life."[11]

"The idea is to invent, design and manufacture a new way to move for global travelers. The vision [is] to rethink personal transportation from the wheel up to the smallest details," Mocellin told *Newz Hook*.[12] Revolve's airless tire, with its modular structure, also can be used on other vehicles, such as bicycles, land drones, and carts.

Patience is key. Mocellin developed hundreds of 3D models and prototypes to find the most efficient folding mechanism. Revolve Air's wheels also are puncture-proof. The gap Mocellin filled is clear. And because Mocellin is an excellent industrial designer, the chair is aesthetically pleasing as well.

And guess what? As it turns out, Mocellin did reinvent the wheel. Revolve Air uses modular, foldable, hexagonally structured wheels!

DEI and Creativity

Whether you're an individual or part of a team, an organization, or a company, diversity, equity, and inclusion matter. Research shows exposure to multiple cultures in and of itself can enhance creativity.[13]

Social psychologist Adam Galinsky, the Paul Calello Professor of Leadership and Ethics at the Columbia Business School, has conducted extensive research supporting the claim that diversity yields creativity and innovative thinking. In one study, Galinsky and his colleagues found that people who have deep relationships with someone from another country become more creative and score higher on routine creativity tests.[14] In a field study, Galinsky and his colleagues studied esteemed fashion designers from major fashion houses who had immersed themselves in different cultures. They found the time spent in a different culture "predicted their entire fashion line creativity."[15]

In 1998 the American cellist Yo-Yo Ma conceived Silkroad, an ensemble of diverse musicians. Silkroad is "a model for cultural collaboration—for the exchange of ideas, tradition, and innovation across borders."[16]

In Ma's speech "Art for Life's Sake," he used a biology metaphor to make an important point about diversity, which he called "the edge effect." Ma gave an illuminating example of creativity from ecology. At the point of intersection, where two ecosystems meet, such as the forest and the savannah, is the site of "edge effect." "In that transition zone, because of the influence the two ecological communities have on each other, you find the greatest diversity of life, as well as the greatest number of new life forms."[17]

Ma explained: "The edge effect is where those of varied backgrounds come together in a zone of transition; a region of less structure, more diversity and more possibility. The edge is a time and place of transformation and movement."[18]

You've just seen how individuals who thought about inclusion and equity formed their worthwhile ideas, setting goals, finding gaps, and seeing gains. Research shows that diversity within corporations and organizations promotes creativity.[19] The most common assumption is that simply bringing people of different back-grounds and cultures to the table enhances a group's creativity. Some research, however, says that it goes beyond that: in a diverse group, people anticipate differences of opinion or differing per-spectives or beliefs and work harder to prepare their research and rationales, which enhances discussions overall.[20]

DEI in Teams and Companies

We have seen how looking at the Three Gs from others' perspec-tives will amplify your thinking by revealing issues and points you might not have considered. Research points to perspective taking as an important mechanism to unlock diversity's potential for team creativity.[21]

There is also a business case to be made for diversity and inclu-sion. Companies that are more diverse than their peers are more likely to outperform on profitability. And, according to a recent report from McKinsey, the greater the diversity, the higher the like-lihood of outperforming their peers:

> Companies with more than 30 percent women executives were more likely to outperform companies where this percentage ranged from 10 to 30....A substantial differential likelihood of outperformance—48 percent—separates the most from the least gender-diverse companies.
>
> In the case of ethnic and cultural diversity, our business-case findings are equally compelling....As we have previously found, the likelihood of outperformance continues to be higher for diversity in ethnicity than for gender.[22]

To build high-performance teams, "look for 'cognitive' diver-sity, which is mixing people together with different thinking styles, habits and perspectives," advises research firm Gartner. The firm goes on to advise "Diversity is the first and easier step, but inclusion is the key to leveraging diversity."[23]

There are ways to go about working on diverse teams to amplify the Three Gs. When seeking ideas that are worthwhile and not just profitable, we must initiate dialogue and not debate. This demands more than simply assembling a diverse group. "Companies will not reap benefits from diversity unless they build a culture that insists on equality."[24] Once again, a way to do that is to understand others' perspectives and other points of view. When I interviewed Donald R. Marks, associate professor of psychology at Kean University, he told me about the work of Lisa Schirch and David Campt, who published a book that he highly recommends to everyone, especially people in leadership positions—*The Little Book of Dialogue for Difficult Subjects.*

Marks explained,

> The framework draws crucial distinctions between "debate" and "dialogue." As the authors note, debate is conducted with winning in mind, even if that means discrediting the views of others. The aim of dialogue, by contrast, is understanding another's perspective. When one listens to another person in the context of debate, one does so to find holes or flaws in the counterargument. In dialogue one listens to understand how other people have arrived at their perspectives and beliefs. . . . Dialogue favors trust and collaboration as participants share their views and work toward shared understanding.[25]

I asked Rich Tu, group creative director at JKR, "What are five essential questions about power, identity, intersectionality, appropriation, dehumanization, and systemic racism that business people should ask when critiquing and judging strategies or creative ideas?" Tu responded with the following:

1. During this process, was there an opportunity for everyone to contribute?

2. For this solution to win, does someone have to lose?

3. Is this community telling their story?

4. Would I be proud to take a snapshot of this "table" I've set?

5. Most importantly, Who are we missing?[26]

Responsibility and Allyship

If you elect to tell someone else's story, you have a responsibility to be an ally.

In his animated film *Flee*, director and writer Jonas Poher Rasmussen tells the story of his close friend, Amin (whom he's known since high school in Denmark), who fled Kabul as a child with his family during the 1980s to seek asylum in Scandinavia. (Amin is not Rasmussen's friend's real name. Rasmussen elected to keep his friend's identity hidden.) As a director, Rasmussen behaves as an ally and employs the medium of animation to creatively tell another person's story in a responsible yet authentic manner. Animation allows an artist to remove us one step from reality yet convey a narrative we can relate to.

Rasmussen had set a goal of telling Amin's story when the two men were in their twenties, and he waited for Amin to be ready to tell it. Rasmussen wanted to tell his friend's personal story, but when the 2015 migrant crisis erupted in Europe, both filmmaker and subject felt the story had to reflect this new reality.

"I felt the need to give the refugees we saw on the highways in Denmark and the rest of Europe a human face...and show that being a refugee is not an identity. It's a life circumstance," Rasmussen said.[27]

When we employ the Three Gs for art, whether visual arts, literature, music, drama, poetry, or any unconventional art form, it is often more challenging to point out the gap but easier to point out the gain because people inevitably respond, and the work resonates. In the case of *Flee*, Kim Skotte, the film editor for the Danish newspaper *Politiken*, sums it up: "For Danes now it's becoming the kind of film that you have to see if you want to know what's going on. That's very, very different from being oh, another heavy documentary about refugees."[28]

In his acceptance speech for the 2021 Nordic Council Film Prize, a prestigious annual award given by the region's parliamentary body, the director implied his goal, gap, and gain. "When we talk about refugees today, it soon becomes a discussion about who is for and against refugees," he said. "But I hope *Flee* will remind people how important it is that we continue to turn to each other."[29]

"Where Are You Really From?" and Other Microaggressions

Throughout my career, I have heard an occasional person ask another, "Can I touch your hair?" or "Where are you really from?" By looking through the DEI lens, ad agency Droga5 created a campaign that supercharges the Three Gs.

How many times must Asian Americans respond to the question, "Where are you really from?" To counter bias, Droga5 created the pro bono "Really From" project, a series of special "travel posters" for the Asian American Federation, a public advocacy group. Each poster spotlights a personal story from community members, including Instagram fashion partnerships director Eva Chen, novelist Kevin Kwan, speed skater Apolo Ohno, and victims of anti-Asian hate crimes such as Noel Quintana. Each subject was illustrated by a different Asian American artist and promotes a city, such as Houston, New York, and San Diego—because that's where these folks are really from.

As a Filipino American, Droga5 art director Nod Arceo McFall had multiple experiences with racial microaggressions on both U.S. coasts. These encounters led him to the idea for this campaign. McFall told *Muse* about an exchange with a "Caucasian" nurse in a midtown Manhattan physician's office. Although McFall told the nurse the name of the city in Washington State where he was raised, she still asked, "But where are you really from?" "The commonality in which AAPI [Asian American Pacific Islander] folks encounter this question is ubiquitous, and really is a sign that many in the United States still associate Asian Americans as a population to be 'other-ed.' It signals to AAPI people that in some ways, we are still not welcome in the country that many of us were born and raised in."[30]

Kevin Nadal, professor of psychology at John Jay College of Criminal Justice, told Andrew Limbong of NPR:

> Microaggressions are defined as the everyday, subtle, intentional— and oftentimes unintentional—interactions or behaviors that communicate some sort of bias toward historically marginalized groups. The difference between microaggressions and overt discrimination or macroaggressions, is that people who commit microaggressions might not even be aware of them....Oftentimes, people don't even realize that they're doing those sorts of things. And in fact, if you were to stop them and say, "Why did you just move?" They would deny it because they don't recognize that their behaviors communicate their racial biases.[31]

When I teach, I present DEI as a surefire way to magnify the power of the Three Gs. To fulfill her senior passion project assignment in my design course, Danielle Thomas, now a professional designer, created a short film titled *Pretty for a Black Girl.* The film deals with microaggressions against Black women today. Kean University aired Thomas's film during our annual Research Days conference. After the film was shown, dozens of women in the audience rushed up to Thomas to praise her work and say how the film's message resonated with them. Thomas was talking to them about something they were living. Stereotypes related to race, ethnicity, gender, age, sexuality, or to people living with disabilities, prejudice woven into policies, social injustice, systemic racism, bigoted rhetoric, and conspiracy narratives all likely fuel potential offenders' acts.

Let's look at *Pretty for a Black Girl* through the lens of the Three Gs. Thomas's *goal* was to illuminate microaggressions against Black women. There was a *gap* in film about this subject. The *gains* are raising awareness, educating potential offenders, and encouraging dialogue.

UNLOCK YOUR CREATIVE POTENTIAL

After completing this chapter, here are your action steps:

Think not only about how diversity, equity, and inclusion amplify the Three Gs, but also about how exclusion and bias amplify social injustice. Answering these questions will set you on the path to ensuring diversity, equity, and inclusion. Ask:

- Have I considered the viewpoints of others in determining my goal?

- Have I supercharged the Three Gs by taking multiple perspectives?

- For my idea to succeed, does someone or some group have to lose?

- When working on a diverse team, have I used the Three Gs?

- Is it possible to shift or evolve a goal so that a more diverse group will gain?

- When working on a diverse and inclusive team, have I had a dialogue with my teammates?

- Do I have an opportunity to explore another culture, to learn, and to be immersed in that culture?

- Do I have an opportunity to elevate equity?

How you frame your goal, or reframe it once you've set it, can make a world of difference to your progress. Framing and reframing can take lots of forms. For instance, "I want to reinvent the wheel" is by any measure a lofty goal. When Mocellin reframed it as "I want to reinvent a wheel for a foldable wheelchair," he generated a great idea. Take time to see if you can reframe your goal—or reframe your question. Changing a frame allows you to see the goal from different points of view.

BUILD A CREATIVE HABIT

Be receptive to different viewpoints or opinions. Listen and don't shut down when someone else's view doesn't line up with your own. I'm not suggesting you need to listen to misinformation or the ramblings of people who are ignorant; rather, be open to new experiences and to what intelligent people and experts have to say. Engage in dialogue not debate.

Think about being willing to revise your thinking or views. Be open rather than overconfident or stubborn, and separate your specific point of view from your sense of self. Being open to new methods and new experiences (whether it's a cuisine you've never tried or a point of view you've never considered) or being curious about a diverse range of others' views—all set you up for inspiration.

For example, spatial ideas in the woodcut prints by Japanese artists of the *ukiyo-e* school influenced the work of impressionist Claude Monet. Monet didn't appropriate; he was open to different ideas about depicting spatial illusion other than the ones conventionally employed in Western European modern art. Listen and engage respectfully.

When you are working toward generating an idea with a group of people, try using "Yes, and…" It's an improv tool that encourages the participants to accept what their partner has said ("Yes,") and build on it ("and…"); it works well to keep a discussion flowing respectfully, without shutting anyone's suggestions down. "Yes, and…" challenges people to move a discussion forward, avoiding negativity and perhaps bias in a corporate setting.

"Seeing Something in a New Way Is Seeing It for the First Time" is a prompt Richard Wilde, professor, creativity expert, creative director, and author, would give to his students in a visual thinking course at the School of Visual Arts in New York City.[32] That's what perspective taking does as well.

NOTES: YOUR IDEAS

To unlock your creative potential, think of ways you could learn about different cultures. I suggest a virtual or actual visit to an art or anthropology museum to see a collection you've never seen. For example, the following museums offer virtual visits:

Louvre: https://collections.louvre.fr/en/

Smithsonian: https://www.si.edu/museums

Tokyo National Museum: https://www.tnm.jp/

CHAPTER 7

EMOTIONAL OBSTACLES

Never be limited by other people's
limited imaginations.
MAE JEMISON, AMERICAN ENGINEER,
PHYSICIAN, AND FORMER NASA ASTRONAUT

When my daughter was a toddler, she preferred to eat penne pasta because it was the only one that would stay on her fork. Keeping spaghetti on her fork, not to mention pronouncing it, was frustrating. The skill of managing a forkful of spaghetti does take patience, a trait many toddlers don't possess.

Enter Dan Pashman, the host of the James Beard Award–winning podcast *Sporkful*. Pashman's *goal* was to make the ideal pasta shape. What would make it ideal according to Pashman? It would have to have three characteristics: (1) forkability (how easy it is to get the shape on your fork and keep it there), (2) sauceability (how readily sauce adheres to the shape), and (3) toothsinkability (how satisfying it is to sink your teeth into it).[1]

"I came at this from an outsider's perspective," Pashman explained to Dom Nero of *Esquire*. "I'm not a chef, I'm not Italian-American, I'm not a pasta expert or historian, so I tried to embrace that perspective, you know? I just approached it from the perspective of someone who loves to eat pasta."

Nero wrote, "Pashman made it sound so simple on the phone: 'What's the pasta shape that I would most want to eat that doesn't exist?'"[2]

However, if you listen to Pashman's podcast episodes on the subject, "Mission ImPASTAble," you learn that his original ideas for pasta shapes were crushed; no one wanted to distribute his pasta until the Brooklyn-based artisan food company Sfoglini came along. What's more, Pashman invested a great deal of his own money.

"There were so many emotional ups and downs," he told Ashlie D. Stevens of *Salon* in a recent interview. "You will hear my wife running out of patience with this whole mission. My kids are part of it. I'm literally brought to tears on more than one occasion. You will learn a ton about how pasta is made, why this project took nearly three years, and you will laugh hysterically, because a lot of things go wrong in very, very funny ways."[3]

You read that correctly. It took Pashman three years to bring his *goal* of perfect pasta, called cascatelli (Italian for "waterfalls"), to life. He saw a *gap*—maximizing the three qualities by which all pasta should be judged, according to Pashman. People evidently see a *gain* because Pashman now can't manufacture it fast enough to keep up with demand.

There are obstacles that can get in anyone's way when trying to generate an idea—even when a terrific framework such as the Three Gs is in place. Some external obstacles might be obvious—working full-time, a family to care for, a companion who wants your time, inadequate resources, and much more. I will offer suggestions to help with these in a bit. But for many people, one big internal obstacle is impatience. That's why I told you Pashman's story.

Please be patient with yourself. Creativity and actualizing an idea take time. Hang in there. As I said before, your present self might be frustrated but your future self will be very pleased you stuck with it.

What's more, at times, a goal can be born out of adversity. Listen to Hwang Dong-hyuk's story.

SPOTLIGHT   NETFLIX'S *SQUID GAME*

Hwang Dong-hyuk and his family were struggling financially in 2009, when the global financial crisis hit South Korea. He couldn't secure financing for the film he was working on. His mother had retired. He, his mother, and grandmother all resorted to taking out loans.

In an interview with the *Guardian*, Hwang told Stuart Jeffries that he frequented Seoul's comic book cafes.

> "I read *Battle Royal* and *Liar Game* and other survival game comics.
> I related to the people in them, who were desperate for money and
> success. That was a low point in my life. If there was a survival game
> like these in reality, I wondered, would I join it to make money for
> my family? I realized that, since I was a filmmaker, I could put my
> own touch to these kinds of stories so I started on the script."[4]

A filmmaker, he originally envisioned *Squid Game* as a film. Drawing upon the games children play, such as tug-of-war; red light; green light; and the titular game, the squid game (which Hwang played as a child), Hwang set out to write about "desperate people who sign up to play mysterious children's games in the hopes of winning a large cash prize" (Netflix).

In the real-life version of the squid game, a physically demanding game, players are divided into two teams: attackers and defenders. Attackers advance their way through a squid-shaped area drawn on the ground while defenders try to stop them. But in Hwang's imaginary world, *Squid Game* is a dystopian survival drama, where 456 down-and-out contestants compete for a prize in potentially lethal children's games.

Bringing *Squid Game* to the screen was a challenging journey. Although Hwang finished the screenplay in 2009, he couldn't secure investors or a cast. People thought it was too complex and not commercial enough. He moved on to other successful film projects: *Silenced* (2011), *Miss Granny* (2014), and *The Fortress* (2017).

Approximately ten years after generating the idea for *Squid Game*, Hwang Dong-hyuk worked with Netflix to actualize it. Netflix afforded him creative freedom, and he expanded his story into a series. His goal as he worked on the project was to "rank No 1 on the Netflix U.S. chart for at least a day."[5] *Squid Game* has proved to be much more successful than Hwang had hoped.

Hwang's *goal* was to write a screenplay to convey a message about modern capitalism. He filled a *gap* that resonated with a global audience. The *gain*? Netflix has a hit. Hwang has a hit. And hopefully the audience will have a greater understanding that the overall global economic order is painfully unequal.

Although the squid game is a South Korean children's game, Hwang believes the message is universal. A Netflix story on the background of the series explains:

> The series examines human nature and how we change from childhood to adulthood through showing adults revisit and play children's games. Director Hwang Dong-hyuk shared, "I wanted to write a story that was an allegory or fable about modern capitalist society, something that depicts an extreme competition, somewhat like the extreme competition of life." It's not all depressing though, as we see the characters hold onto their humanity and hope. The commentary on human nature and society is definitely thought-provoking.[6]

Overcoming Obstacles

We've come to the penultimate chapter of this book, and I want to make sure you feel—yes, feel—you're ready. Emotions play a great part in how we act. In this chapter I'm going to prime your emotional side to prepare you to ideate.

Internal and external obstacles can prevent us from setting a goal and eventually generating an idea. As an educator, I don't let obstacles stop my students from succeeding. Try these tools I have used effectively over the years with thousands of university seniors and with the faculty and business executives I mentor.

Make a Deal with Yourself

When I mentor design faculty from universities all over the United States and the world about nonfiction research and writing, one of the most oft-asked questions is, How do you manage to find the time to write?

My answer is always the same: My time devoted to writing is nonnegotiable. I explain: There are things I do that are nonnegotiable. I don't negotiate with myself about brushing my teeth, showering, eating vegetables, or exercising. I just do those things with no arguments. (There are things I do negotiate with myself about that I shouldn't, such as how many cookies per day, but that's another story.) But time devoted to writing is nonnegotiable.

Sound silly? I don't waste time arguing with myself, and I don't let myself off the hook. Imagine all the times I could say to myself, *I could take a dance class instead of writing*, or, *I could binge watch that new series everyone is talking about*. Nope. That's all avoided.

For some people, establishing a time of day to work on a project, write, or ideate is important to help them keep to their schedule. Figure out what works for you, and make it nonnegotiable. No arguments.

Make a commitment. You likely will encounter obstacles along the way but think of how satisfied you'll feel if you've made the time you need to realize your idea.

Tackle Your Doubts

Self-doubt is a very real feeling. We live in a society where there is great pressure to achieve. And all the examples in this book are impressive. Not everyone is interested in the same things, nor are they capable of the same things. However, everyone can generate a worthwhile or even a great idea using the Three Gs.

I am glad Mocellin designed the Revolve Air portable wheelchair because I'm not capable of inventing it, nor am I interested in generating an idea for the perfect pasta, but I have generated good ideas for short stories as well as ideas for ad campaigns and designs, among other things. But if harnessing electricity had been up to me, we'd be sitting in the dark.

There's a tendency to inflate self-doubts. Here's a way to combat that. Jot down one thing that's bothering you—that's standing in your way of generating your idea. First determine whether it is a legitimate reason or whether it is a mental barrier you can overcome. Write down how you can overcome it. Also, try to determine what triggers self-doubt. Then you can resolve to do something about it.

Here's another strategy for combating self-doubt. Replace any negative self-talk with a more productive narrative. It might feel manufactured at first; however, it will help you vanquish those pesky negative thoughts. For example, if one of my clients were to reject my design proposals, instead of thinking, *I guess I blew that,* I would reframe my self-talk to, *I welcome a challenge to generate new design concepts.* (And I would take a dance class to blow off steam.)

Focus

If you work full time, perhaps you can dedicate a half hour to your idea every day, or at least every other day. That way, it will be in your brain, and your subconscious will be working on it even when you're not paying full attention to it. When you're sitting on a park bench or showering, for example, your goal, the gap, or a gain may take form.

When you're taking the time to work with the Three Gs or work with the idea you've generated, focus on it. Filter out distractions. Let that be the one project you work on for however long you've decided to dedicate to it for the day. Prioritize your projects. It's a good way to work on what's most urgent first and move down the priorities list from there. But it's also good to give full attention to your idea. That doesn't mean you have to sit at your desk and force yourself to think. As I mentioned earlier, subconscious thinking happens during an incubation period or when you're performing semi-conscious activities, such as strolling in the park or folding laundry.

Change Your Thinking

Here's a great piece of advice to deal with obstacles and to unlock creative potential, whether your hurdle relates to your own skills or talent, the project, or the circumstances—change or reframe your thinking.

Ask yourself, How can I look at this in a different way? Can I look at this scenario, situation, object, setting, or relationship through a different lens? Or, can you obtain someone else's vantage point, someone quite different from yourself? When you're with colleagues or team members, obtain multiple perspectives on your research or findings.

Before you reframe, jot down what you're thinking—your goal or your notions, a tentative goal, your concerns, your thoughts, your feelings, and so on. Now you've acknowledged not only what you're thinking but a possible goal. If there's any negative or pedestrian thinking in there, you have something to reframe.

Check what you've written for what's subjective (are you being hard on yourself?) and what's objective (what would a wise friend or colleague say when viewing your goal?). Try to stick to facts and be objective. Your thinking should be helpful, not detrimental.

Reframing also can be subtle. People often think they must be their own coach: "Yeah, you're brilliant! Go get 'em, tiger!" Often it's more useful to be pragmatic and think incrementally. For instance, think, *This goal will take time, and I have the determination and intelligence to carry this out. I will take it G by G.*

Before we move on to how reframing unlocks creative potential, one more piece of advice. Reframing can help you find meaning— that is, find the gap and the gain. Think of how Mocellin realized the gap by speaking with Paralympians and found great meaning in reinventing the wheel for a portable and sturdy wheelchair that would make a lot of lives much better.

And you can also find meaning in the Three Gs process itself. I love to generate ideas because it actually produces feel-good chemicals in my brain; once I get into thinking for a period, there's a flow. You can find satisfaction in the process of thinking something through.

Reframing a question can change outcomes. In the TED Talk "Choice, Happiness, and Spaghetti Sauce," journalist and writer Malcolm Gladwell explained how reframing a problem can lead to successful solutions. Prego, in its pursuit of the perfect spaghetti sauce, hired Howard R. Moskowitz, an experimental psychologist who worked in the field of psychophysics. Although Prego was looking for the perfect spaghetti sauce, Moskowitz reframed the assignment based on his data: there is no one perfect spaghetti sauce, only different kinds of spaghetti sauce that suit different kinds of people. Instead of trying to please everyone with one sauce, Prego heeded Moskowitz's advice and created a varied spaghetti sauce product line that generated hundreds of millions of dollars in sales.

Reframing a problem can change outcomes. Early in my teaching career, I noticed greater absenteeism at certain times of the academic year. To reduce absenteeism, I decided to make the students *not* want to miss a class because the classes were so exciting and interesting. I didn't punish absenteeism—I made them not want to miss out. To this day, when I say, "I might cancel a class," the students inevitably say, "Oh, no! Please don't!" Well, most of them.

UNLOCK YOUR CREATIVE POTENTIAL

After completing this chapter, here are your action steps:

Think about how you can overcome any emotional obstacles that might interfere with using the Three Gs to generate, crystallize, or unlock an idea. Answering these questions will set you on a personally rewarding journey to unlock your creativity:

- Can you clear your path of (at least some) obstacles so you can realize your idea?

- Can you maximize your energy by focusing on your idea?

- Can you figure out where you can find support, even if it's someone who can take over a small chore?

- Can you envision what you want and stay positive about it? (Don't let negativity—your own or others'—infiltrate your goal.)

BUILD A CREATIVE HABIT

Be resilient. Accept that we all fail from time to time. Things go wrong. Most initiatives take time, resources, research, iterations, support, and determination.

The beauty of the Three Gs is that it's a process, a system, that involves thoughtfulness. That is not a guarantee against failure. Many ideas require funding, family support, administrative support, and so on. No scientist starts an experiment knowing the outcome. I know scientists who have repeated the same experiment many times.

A quick anecdote: I had negotiated a book contract with a publisher with whom I had published previously. I negotiated well and signed the contract. Two weeks later, I received an email saying that the publisher had canceled my contract. It seemed that the person who negotiated had agreed to too high a royalty and the higher-ups decided against publishing the book. What? OK. No point in arguing. I visited LinkedIn and searched for senior editors. I found one whose publishing list fit my book and messaged her. I signed a contract with her publishing house within a week, and they published my book. I could have moped, but I was determined. (I did indulge in a few extra cookies.)

Just keep moving forward.

NOTES: YOUR IDEAS

Emotional obstacles, such as fear of failure, redirect your energy away from your goal or idea. Situations, such as being overworked, also affect you. If this is the case,

- What is the situation that is interfering with working on your idea?

- What about this situation do you find challenging?

- What is one action that you could take to mitigate the situation in order to move your idea forward?

YOUR IDEA

I always did something I was a little not ready to do. I think
that's how you grow. When there's that moment of "Wow,
I'm not really sure I can do this," and you push through
those moments, that's when you have a breakthrough.

MARISSA MAYER, COFOUNDER, SUNSHINE

Getting started. Does it sound odd to end a book with "Getting started"?

One of the biggest hurdles to doing anything is getting started. In her book *The Creative Habit*, choreographer Twyla Tharp says she starts her day with a ritual workout; by making it a routine, she has habitualized the workout.[1] Make getting started a ritual. My friend Richard, a literature professor and novelist, always writes the first sentence of a new paragraph before he ends his writing for the day so that he will have somewhere to start the next day.

You have what you need to use the Three Gs. The New Art of Ideas works: Set a *goal*. Determine if there's a *gap* you can fill. See if there would be a *gain*.

The Three Gs of my ideation system help you break it down. Don't worry about all three at once. Take it G by G.

If you're having difficulty setting a goal, make a list of five goals that interest you the most—small or big or unconventional. Then circle three that make your heart beat a little faster. Don't think about the others anymore.

Now of those three goals, determine which one might have a gap and a gain. No idea is too small if there's a gain in it for someone, society, creatures, or our planet.

Once you've formed a goal and realized a gap and a gain, you're on your way to a worthwhile idea.

The New Art of Ideas Handy Checklist

You can use the Three Gs in any order. A goal isn't the only entry point for an idea. You can start by noticing a gap and move forward from there. Or you may observe a gain, something beneficial to individuals, society, or our planet, and move ahead from that point. The Three Gs framework is nonlinear and fluid. The goal, gap, and gain influence each other—they are not siloed. The Three Gs also allow you to backtrack and reassess.

Start with a Goal

Goal + Gap + Gain → Worthwhile Idea

- ☐ Set a *goal.* Think about what you want to do. Your goal is not your idea—it's only the start.
- ☐ Find a *gap.* See if your goal will fill a void, a need that has not yet been met.
- ☐ Determine a *gain,* which provides a benefit to individuals, a community, society, creatures big or small, or our planet.

Start with a Gap

Gap + Gain + Goal → Worthwhile Idea

☐ If you notice a *gap*, find out if there is a need to fill that void.

☐ Determine what the *gain* would be and how many people it would serve or how it would benefit society or our planet.

☐ Set your *goal*. Think about what you want to achieve.

Start with a Gain

Gain + Gap + Goal → Worthwhile Idea

☐ You observe a *gain*, the potential good in something—a benefit for individuals, a community, society, creatures, or our planet.

☐ Determine if the benefit fills a *gap*, a need that has not yet been met, whether in a sector or a discipline or for an underserved audience.

☐ Set a *goal*. Think about what you want to accomplish.

Employing the Three Gs should allow you to generate many ideas and even better ideas.

Your Ideas

An idea doesn't exist until you form it. You might set a goal and then stop for a while only to come back to it later. That's OK. You might change your goal, and that's OK too. You've read examples of people who've done that with great outcomes. Even with the Three Gs, generating an idea takes effort and focus. Once you've generated an idea, put it on screen or on paper. Put it out in the world—you've built something.

Ideas are constructions. Ideas are seeds—your idea might inspire someone else. Ideas often connect to other ideas, and they connect us to each other.

I look forward to hearing about how you've used the Three Gs to generate your ideas. Because worthwhile ideas can alter the course of human progress.

UNLOCK YOUR CREATIVE POTENTIAL

In conclusion, here are your action steps:

Think about using the Three Gs to generate, crystallize, or unlock an idea. Take a look at the 17 Sustainable Development Goals from the United Nations: (1) No Poverty; (2) Zero Hunger; (3) Good Health and Well-being; (4) Quality Education; (5) Gender Equality; (6) Clean Water and Sanitation; (7) Affordable and Clean Energy; (8) Decent Work and Economic Growth; (9) Industry, Innovation, and Infrastructure; (10) Reduced Inequalities; (11) Sustainable Cities and Communities; (12) Responsible Consumption and Production; (13) Climate Action; (14) Life below Water; (15) Life on Land; (16) Peace, Justice, and Strong Institutions; and (17) Partnerships for the Goals.[2] Keep them in mind as you go about your daily life. These goals set forth by the U.N. are grand; please think of them as general categories that your specific, smaller-scale goal might fall under.

Answering these questions will set you on a personally rewarding journey to unlock your creativity:

- Can you identify one U.N. Sustainable Development Goal that could match with a goal of your own? With a gap? With a benefit to people, animals, or our planet?

- Can you be patient, taking it G by G to generate or crystallize your idea?

- Can you find a way to get started—for example, make notes while having your morning coffee or tea?

- Does a goal you're thinking about make your heart beat a little faster?

BUILD A CREATIVE HABIT

Be a mindful listener. Great leaders listen carefully. Great teachers listen intently to their students' questions and concerns. John Maeda, American designer, executive, and technologist, recommends story listening. "What I've seen is a leader doesn't start with storytelling, they start with story listening," Maeda said at a Future of Storytelling session that I facilitated.

When you actively listen, not only might someone's comment spark an idea, but you get to know how people feel and what they think. Listening to your target audience often leads to an insight. In general, listening just makes you a better leader and nicer to be around.

If you found this book helpful, I encourage you to connect with me via my website, LinkedIn, or social media. Please consider posting a reader review on your favorite bookselling site. And I am thankful to you for wanting to use the Three Gs to bring worthwhile ideas into the world.

All the best wishes to you for success!

NOTES: YOUR IDEAS

Keep going. Here's why. Your worthwhile idea will...

- make a difference for the better

- inspire someone else's thinking

- make people's lives healthier, safer, easier, more joyful...

The New Art of Ideas
DISCUSSION GUIDE

No matter what goal you want to achieve, *The New Art of Ideas* offers a proven system for how to get worthwhile ideas. The Three Gs framework will teach you precisely how to generate good ideas, ones that benefit individuals, society, and our planet. *The New Art of Ideas* will reshape the way you think about idea generation and offer the tools and strategies you need to transform your thinking—whether you are a team looking to develop a new product, a faculty member who wants to teach your students to ideate, an organization hoping to rethink your sector, or an individual who wishes to invent something, write a story, design an athletic shoe, generate an idea for a business, get more and better ideas on the job, or get any worthwhile idea.

The New Art of Ideas is based on a brand-new framework:

Goal + Gap + Gain → Worthwhile Idea

I divide *The New Art of Ideas* framework into three Gs: goal, gap, and gain. Breaking it down into the Three Gs can help you understand what a worthwhile idea is, how it works, and how to generate one. Always ask if there's a benefit in there for individuals, for society, or for our planet—what do they gain from your goal and from filling this gap? You can use the Three Gs to generate ideas for a community, a company, an entire industry, and so on, to ensure the goal always delivers a gain. If there's no benefit, there's no point in filling a gap—or perhaps there was no gap to begin with.

This is one of the main reasons for you to employ this framework—it yields ideas that move the needle! It generates ideas that are worthwhile, not trivial—ideas that will make a difference because you are seeking an outcome with a benefit for individuals, society, or our planet.

These discussion prompts will engage individuals, teams, and organizations and get them thinking about generating worthwhile ideas.

Individual

1. What goals interest you?

2. What are you passionate about?

3. What do you wish existed in the world to benefit individuals, creatures, society, or our planet?

4. Can you list five goals? Whittle the list down to three goals, then to one goal.

5. Which emotional obstacles most stand in your way? How can you work to eliminate them?

6. What can you do to be more observant of potential gaps and gains?

7. How can you best use your own power, talent, and intelligence to achieve your goal and bring your worthwhile idea to life?

8. What are three things you think would benefit your profession?

9. What are three things you think would benefit your community or society?

10. What are three things you think would benefit our planet?

Teams

1. If you are a team leader, how could you employ the new Three Gs framework with your team?

2. What's the best way for your team to employ the Three Gs when starting with a preset goal? Are you asking enough challenging questions before setting a goal, looking for possible gaps in research or the industry?

3. What's the best way for your team to employ the Three Gs when starting *without* a preset goal?

4. What organizational system will allow your team to conduct research into finding gaps and gains in the industry or discipline?

5. What have your team members observed that would benefit people and that your company could make happen? Can you identify specific gains?

6. How can your team members feel more comfortable speaking up? Do you encourage dialogue and not debate?

7. How can a culture be built for worthwhile results?

8. What is the source of emotional obstacles at the team level?

9. Have you done multiple perspective taking?

10. Have you built inclusive diverse teams?

Organizations

1. Idea generation is an urgent concern in a competitive international marketplace. How relevant are worthwhile ideas to your organization's growth? Please be specific.

2. How do worthwhile ideas and/or innovation (new worthwhile ideas) play a role in your industry or sector?

3. How can leaders guide their organizations in employing the Three Gs? Can they offer guidance on a systemic level?

4. All businesses today are idea-dependent businesses. How can your organization help its C-suite to set goals, seek gaps, and find gains?

5. Have you surveyed employees to gauge their perspectives on diversity, equity, and inclusion in your organization? Are you conducting multiple perspective taking? Is dialogue encouraged?

6. How is leadership fostering a willingness to question goals, seek gaps, and find gains for people?

7. How can your organization's leadership eliminate barriers and emotional obstacles to foster worthwhile ideation?

8. What's the best way for your organization to utilize the Three Gs—starting with a set goal? Seeking a gap? Or pinpointing a gain?

9. When your organization sets goals, who determines if the goals are correct? Are you asking the right questions? Are you asking enough challenging questions before setting a goal— looking for possible gaps in research or the industry?

10. What are ten possible gains for individuals, creatures, society, and our planet that your organization can make happen?

EIGHT WAYS YOU CAN SET YOUR GOAL

When there are no preset demands, goals, or guidelines, let's look at eight ways you can set a goal.

1. Build on an Observation

Keen observation is fundamental to research. There are many ways to set a goal. At times, you happen on it. Make it a practice of being alert to possibilities—an anomaly, an unexpected connection or occurrence, an insight, a recurring theme, and more.

If you notice a gap, investigate. Find out if there is a need to fill that void. Determine what the gain would be and how many people it would serve.

An observation doesn't have to be one that sets a goal in motion. You might observe a gap or a gain—in that case, you start from there.

2. Spot a Problem That Needs Fixing

You're in a unique position to see a problem that needs fixing. Perhaps you're a physical therapist, and you notice what's missing from the equipment sets. Or you're an educator, and you can no longer stand the fact that students sit at a desk for hours at a time.

Noticing pain points is extremely useful. If you search social media to see what people are complaining about, what their pain points are on various topics, products, brands, and so on, you might have an insight into setting a goal, filling a gap, or providing a gain.

3. Follow a Passion

So many great ideas stem from people's passions—their interest in a subject, a hobby, something they do beyond their job, or something they just keep at until it works.

4. Go with What You Know Best

When you are intimately familiar with a discipline or industry, you can see how you might be able to make things easier for people. You'll also be better able to identify gaps, know who is underserved, and see which paths have not yet been explored.

5. Do What Makes Sense for Your Company's Plan, Customers, and the Planet

Identify specifically what your organization can do to contribute to progress for individuals, society, or the planet. What expertise does it have that will lead to worthwhile ideas?

6. Consider Neglected Problems, Endemic Problems, or Urgent Needs

We face so many neglected problems in so many sectors. There is always a need for new ideas and certainly a need for urgent ideas during times of war, famine, pandemic, tsunami, or other acts of nature or human-caused disasters. There are many ideas that can lead to working on excellent goals, such as the Sustainable Development Goals set by the United Nations, for example, ending poverty, bringing about peace, quality education, good health and well-being, clean water and sanitation, social justice, gender equality, clean energy, decent work and wages, economic growth, innovations in infrastructure, reduced inequalities, sustainable cities, responsible production methods, climate action, care for the oceans and all our environments.

You could think of a gap as a neglected problem.

7. Ask "What Else?"

When you're observant, what you see, hear, notice, or investigate might trigger a goal. Ask: What else is possible? What else can you do with this material, data, or observation? What else is there to discover here? Who else can you collaborate with?

8. Ask Yourself What You Wish Existed (or What's Missing?)

This is pretty easy—it's your wish list for making the world just a bit, or a whole lot, better.

HOW DIVERSITY, EQUITY, AND INCLUSION CAN AMPLIFY THE THREE GS

A Discussion Guide for Leaders

To see how diversity, equity, and inclusion (DEI) can amplify the Three Gs and help your organization, assemble a diverse, inclusive team. It's best practice to engage everyone in your organization in dialogue, from interns to managers to the C-suite. It's also advisable to have a representative from your organization's office of equity and inclusion, if one exists, to assist.

Assign a goal or ask the team to suggest a goal. Let the team take it from there, using the Three Gs and this discussion guide to foster a discussion about diversity, equity, and inclusion.

During this discussion, as a leader you should focus on actively listening to what people think and feel about their voices and senses of place in your organization, rather than on a resulting idea.

The United States Institute of Peace has a useful comparison of dialogue and debate, which I highly recommend. Here are a few highlights:

- In a dialogue, one listens to the other side(s) in order to understand, find meaning, and find agreement.

- Dialogue enlarges and possibly changes a participant's point of view.

- Dialogue opens the possibility of reaching a better solution than any of the original solutions.[1]

The following steps can serve as a guide for achieving a fruitful discussion:

1. Ask each person to ask the person next to them to share their perspective on the *goal* under discussion.

2. Ask team members how they think DEI can magnify the company *goal* under discussion.

3. Ask the team if anyone has ever realized a different perspective from someone unlike themselves. What might the *gains* be for their ideas?

4. Start a group discussion about the organization's *goal* and *gap* as it relates to equity. How can DEI magnify the results by better addressing the *gap?*

5. Remind the group that DEI amplifies the Three Gs—that respectful dialogue leads to ideas with greater breadth and depth by exposing you to different perspectives that open up thinking and offer new avenues. Ask each team member to cite a gain that results from opening the *goal* and *gap* to a different point of view.

6. Ask people on the team what they would expect in allyship when putting ideas out into the world.

7. Ask the team to identify the ideas the team proposed that are most amplified by DEI.

RESEARCH TOOLS

Scenario Map and Social Media Research

To build a better understanding of your audience's personal goals, create a scenario map. Fill in the following responses for your target audience.

SCENARIO MAP

AUDIENCE'S PERSONAL GOAL	
ACTIONS THE AUDIENCE IS TAKING TO ACHIEVE THE GOAL	
AUDIENCE'S FEELINGS ABOUT THE GOAL	

Stay focused on the audience. Your goal is to pinpoint what might be a gain for your target audience. This process might reveal a gap as well.

SOCIAL MEDIA RESEARCH

ASSUMPTIONS ABOUT THE GAIN	
ASSUMPTIONS ABOUT THE AUDIENCE	
QUESTION YOUR ASSUMPTIONS	
SOCIAL MEDIA FINDINGS: ARE YOUR ASSUMPTIONS ACCURATE?	

You can also use social media to put your assumptions to the test. Make a list of assumptions about the gain you envision and about the audience. Next, list questions about your assumptions. Head to social media to search for what the audience is saying to see if you're in the ballpark, and list what you find.

OVERCOMING EMOTIONAL OBSTACLES CHECKLIST

The New Art of Ideas offers a new framework—the Three Gs—for generating ideas. I want to make sure you feel—yes, feel—you're ready. Emotions play a great part in how we act. I'm going to prime your emotional side to prepare you to ideate:

- **Make a Deal with Yourself.** Establish a schedule for your project, and keep to it. Make the time devoted to your project nonnegotiable. Know which times of the day work best for you to think critically and creatively, times when you have a good amount of energy.

- **Tackle Your Doubts.** Focus on your goal. Take action, rather than ruminate. Realize we all have self-doubts, and find a way to energize yourself by working toward your goal.

- **Channel a Success**. Think of something you did well, major (business deal) or minor (arranged a great birthday party). Harness that positive memory of accomplishment.

- **Focus.** Try dedicating a certain amount of time every day or every other day to your idea. That way, even when you're not paying full attention to it, your subconscious will be working on it.

- **Change Your Thinking.** To unlock your creative potential, ask: How can I look at this in a different way? Can I look at this scenario, situation, object, setting, or relationship through a different lens? Is there a vantage point I haven't addressed? Take someone else's perspective, someone very different from yourself. Reframe a common scenario.

- **Take a Step Back.** To achieve your goal and realize your idea, you undoubtedly will have to overcome an obstacle. How you react emotionally to an obstacle is a factor. A good skill to build is removing yourself by one. If your friend were experiencing the same, how would you support them? Treat yourself as you would a friend.

- **You Can Generate a Worthwhile Idea.** Idea generation is no longer a mysterious process. Using the Three Gs, you have the capacity to get ideas that will benefit people or our planet, ideas that will move the needle. The Three Gs framework is a fluid system that's as easy to implement as it is to remember. Using the Three Gs, you and I—all of us—can generate worthwhile ideas.

As Albert Szent-Györgyi told his biographer, Ralph Moss, "Think boldly, don't be afraid of making mistakes, don't miss small details, keep your eyes open, and be modest in everything except your aims."

NOTES: YOUR IDEAS

What is an idea you'd like to work on over the next year? How are you working toward realizing that idea today?

_____

_____

_____

_____

_____

_____

_____

Action plan: What needs to be done, in what order, and by when:

_____

_____

_____

_____

_____

_____

_____

NOTES

Introduction

1. Williesha Morris, "Culture: AbleGamers Just Got a Big Win for the Disabled Gaming Community," *Wired*, September 15, 2021, https://www.wired.com/story/ablegamers-million-dollar-birthday-fundraiser/.

2. Jenny Lay-Flurrie, "Ability Summit: Looking Back at 10 Years of Learning at the Annual Ability Summit," Microsoft Accessibility Blog, May 27, 2020, https://blogs.microsoft.com/accessibility/ability-summit-2020/.

3. Matt Hite, "I'm passionate about making a difference," LinkedIn "About," accessed May 16, 2022, https://www.linkedin.com/in/mattehite/.

4. Deborah Bach, "Microsoft Stories: Plugged In," Microsoft: Story Labs, accessed May 28, 2022, https://news.microsoft.com/stories/xbox-adaptive-controller/

5. "Xbox Adaptive Controller, Game Your Way," Xbox, accessed May 16, 2022, https://www.xbox.com/en-US/accessories/controllers/xbox-adaptive-controller.

6. Bach, "Plugged In."

7. "Microsoft 'Changing the Game,'" McCann New York, accessed May 16, 2022, https://www.mccann.com/work/changing-the-game.

8. Amanda Hess, "Critic's Notebook: Hollywood Bets Big on the Bad Entrepreneur," *New York Times*, March 5, 2022, https://www.nytimes.com/2022/03/05/arts/the-dropout-super-pumped-wecrashed-moguls.html?searchResultPosition=2.

Chapter 1. The New Art of Ideas

1. Robert Viagas, "Beach Read to Broadway! How Lin-Manuel Miranda Turned History into *Hamilton*," *Playbill*, August 5, 2015, https://playbill.com/article/beach-read-to-broadway-how-lin-manuel-miranda-turned-a-history-book-into-hamilton-com-355514.

2. Anna Almendrala, "Lin-Manuel Miranda: It's 'No Accident' *Hamilton* Came to Me on Vacation," *HuffPost*, June 23, 2016, https://www.huffpost.com/entry/lin-manuel-miranda-says-its-no-accident-hamilton-inspiration-struck-onvacation_n_576c136ee4b0b489bb0ca7c2.

3. Ron Chernow, *Alexander Hamilton* (New York: Penguin, 2004).

4. Viagas, "Beach Read to Broadway!"

5. Tatianna Schlossberg, "How Fast Fashion Is Destroying the Planet," review of *Fashionopolis: The Price of Fast Fashion and the Future of Clothes*, by Dana Thomas, *New York Times*, September 3, 2019, https://www.nytimes.com/2019/09/03/books/review/how-fast-fashion-is-destroying-the-planet.html.

6. Schlossberg, "How Fast Fashion Is Destroying."

7. "Recycling System 'LOOOP' Helps H&M Transform Unwanted Garments into New Fashion Favorites," H&M, October 7, 2020, https://about.hm.com/news/general-news-2020/recycling-system–looop–helps-h-m-transform-unwanted-garments-i.html.

8. "H&M: Let's Remake: The World's First In-Store Garment-to-Garment Recycling System," AKQA, accessed May 9, 2022, https://www.akqa.com/work/hm/lets-remake/.

9. Elizabeth Segran, "H&M Will Turn Your Ratty Old T-shirt into a Brand New Sweater," *Fast Company*, October 8, 2020, https://www.fastcompany.com/90561368/hm-will-turn-your-ratty-old-t-shirt-into-a-brand-new-sweater.

10. "About Us," The Phluid Project, accessed May 16, 2022, https://thephluidproject.com/pages/the-phluid-project.

11. Guy Raz, "Stasher and Modern Twist: Kat Nouri," *How I Built This*, NPR, November 21, 2021, https://www.npr.org/2021/11/19/1057386872/stasher-and-modern-twist-kat-nouri.

12. Tom Huddleston Jr., "Success: Tofurky's Creator Was Living in a Treehouse When He Invented the Tofu 'Bird' That's Still a Thanksgiving Staple," CNBC, November 28, 2019, https://www.cnbc.com/2019/11/28/tofurky-creator-lived-in-a-treehouse-before-million-dollar-idea.html.

13. Huddleston, "Success: Tofurky's Creator."

Chapter 2. The Three Gs Method

1. Sal Khan, "I Started Khan Academy. We Can Still Avoid an Education Catastrophe," *New York Times*, August 13, 2020, https://www.nytimes.com/2020/08/13/opinion/coronavirus-school-digital.html.

2. Khan, "I Started Khan Academy."

3. "Kean Associate Dean's Drawings Included in Smithsonian Collection," Kean University, news release, October 7, 2019, https://www.kean.edu/news/kean-associate-deans-drawings-included-smithsonian-collection.

4. "Kean Associate Dean's Drawings."

5. "Who We Are," Surgical Theater, accessed May 16, 2022, https://surgicaltheater.com/who-we-are/.

6. "Who We Are," Surgical Theater.

7. "About Royalty Exchange: Our Mission," Royalty Exchange, accessed May 16, 2022, https://www.royaltyexchange.com/about-royalty-exchange.

8. "Anthony Martini Named CEO of Royalty Exchange," *Music Business Worldwide*, March 11, 2021, https://www.musicbusinessworldwide.com/anthony-martini-named-ceo-of-royalty-marketplace-royalty-exchange/.

9. "Interview: Tiya Miles," *South Writ Large*, Winter 2022, https://southwritlarge.com/articles/interview-5/.

10. Hamilton Cain, "Here are the Winners of the 2021 National Book Awards," *Oprah Daily*, November 18, 2021, https://www.oprahdaily.com/entertainment/books/g38282030/national-book-award-2021-winners/.

11. Our Most Anticipated Books of 2022: *All That She Carried*, Penguin Random House, accessed May 16, 2022, https://www.penguinrandomhouse.com/books/606278/all-that-she-carried-by-tiya-miles/.

12. "Case Study: MTA: The Next Generation of Transit Maps," Work & Co., accessed May 16, 2022, https://work.co/clients/mta/.

13. Howard Markel, "The Real Story behind Penicillin," PBS *NewsHour*, September 27, 2013, https://www.pbs.org/newshour/health/the-real-story-behind-the-worlds-first-antibiotic.

14. "Our Research," Dove, accessed May 9, 2022, https://www.dove.com/us/en/stories/about-dove/our-research.html.

15. Stephen Lepitak, "Burger King UK Announces Plastic Toy Amnesty with 'The Meltdown,'" *The Drum*, September 18, 2019, https://www.thedrum.com/news/2019/09/18/burger-king-uk-announces-plastic-toy-amnesty-with-the-meltdown.

16. Lepitak, "Burger King UK."

17. Lilly Smith, "The Biggest Rebrands of the Decade Have This Visionary Designer behind Them," *Fast Company*, June 9, 2021, https://www.fastcompany.com/90644265/the-biggest-rebrands-of-the-decade-have-this-visionary-designer-in-common.

18. Smith, "The Biggest Rebrands."

19. Armin Vit, "New Logo, Identity, and Package Design for Chobani Done In-house: Get Me to the Greek," Brand New, November 29, 2017, https://www.underconsideration.com/brandnew/archives/new_logo_identity_and_packaging_for_chobani_done_in_house.php.

20. "Work: Crane," Collins, accessed June 26, 2022, https://www.wearecollins.com/work/crane/.

21. Jenny Brewer, "The Crane Paper Company Rebrand by Collins Looks to Art Nouveau for Its Elegant Graphics," It's Nice That, December 7, 2020, https://www.itsnicethat.com/news/collins-crane-paper-company-identity-graphic-design-071220.

22. "Burger King: The Whopper Detour," 2020 Gold Marketing Innovation Solutions, Effie, accessed May 9, 2022, https://www.effie.org/case_database/case/US_2020_E-5696-571.

23. Aria Nouri, "Penicillin and the Importance of Observation," *Scientia* blog, May 3, 2011, American Association for the Advancement of Science, https://www.aaas.org/penicillin-and-importance-observation.

24. "A Dream 33 Years in the Making, Starbucks to Open in Italy," Starbucks Stories and News, February 28, 2016, https://stories.starbucks.com/stories/2016/howard-schultz-dream-fulfilled-starbucks-to-open-in-italy/.

25. "We Believe in a Better Way," OXO, accessed May 16, 2022, https://www.oxo.com/aboutus#:~:text=At%20OXO%2C%20we%20look%20at,problems%20ountil%20we%20osolve%20othem.

26. "Nightmares and Night Terrors," Johns Hopkins Medicine, accessed May 16, 2022, https://www.hopkinsmedicine.org/health/conditions-and-diseases/nightmares-and-night-terrors.

27. Pablo Briñol, Margarita Gascó Rivas, Richard Petty, and Javier Horcajo, "Treating Thoughts As Material Objects Can Increase or Decrease Their Impact on Evaluation," *Psychological Science* 24, no. 1 (2012): 41–47, 10.1177/0956797612449176, https://pubmed.ncbi.nlm.nih.gov/23184587/.

28. Amy Phillips, "Mastercard's 'True Name' Campaign Is Real Corporate Allyship," *OutFront Magazine*, July 8, 2021, https://www.outfrontmagazine.com/mastercards-true-name-campaign-is-real-corporate-allyship/.

29. Kim Bhasin, "How Nike Created Hands-Free Sneakers for People with Disabilities," *Bloomberg*, September 21, 2021, https://www.bloomberg.com/news/articles/2021-09-21/how-nike-nke-created-go-flyease-sneaker-for-people-with-disabilities.

30. "Facts and Figures about Materials, Waste and Recycling: Furniture and Furnishings," U.S. Environmental Protection Agency, accessed May 16, 2022, https://www.epa.gov/facts-and-figures-about-materials-waste-and-recycling/durable-goods-product-specific-data#FurnitureandFurnishings.

31. "From Pre-Loved to Re-Loved: We're Giving IKEA Furniture a Second Life," Ikea, accessed May 16, 2022, https://www.ikea.com/es/en/this-is-ikea/sustainable-everyday/from-pre-loved-to-re-loved-were-giving-ikea-furniture-a-secondlife-pub9e5d35e0.

32. "From Pre-Loved to Re-Loved," Ikea.

33. Scott Carlton, "The Prescription Pill Bottle," Creativepool, accessed May 16, 2022, https://creativepool.com/scott-carlton/projects/the-prescription-paper-pill-bottle-for-tikkun-olam-makers-tom.

34. "An Idea That Stuck: How George deMestral Invented the Velcro Brand Fastener," Velcro, November 11, 2016, https://www.velcro.com/blog/2016/11/an-idea-that-stuck-how-george-de-mestral-invented-the-velcro-fastener/.

35. "Albert Szent-Gyorgyi: Biographical Overview," National Library of Medicine, accessed May 16, 2022, https://profiles.nlm.nih.gov/spotlight/wg /feature/biographical-overview.

Chapter 3. Goal

1. Alice George, "Thank This World War II–Era Film Star for Your WiFi," *Smithsonian Magazine*, April 4, 2019, https://www.smithsonianmag.com /smithsonian-institution/thank-world-war-ii-era-film-star-your-wi-fi-180971584/.

2. Guy Raz, "Back to the Roots: Nikhil Arora and Alejandro Velez," *How I Built This*, NPR, November 8, 2021, https://www.npr.org/2021/11/05 /1052897064/back-to-the-roots-nikhil-arora-and-alejandro-velez.

3. Neil Gaiman, "Where Do You Get Your Ideas?" Neil Gaiman, accessed May 16, 2022, https://www.neilgaiman.com/Cool_Stuff/Essays/Essays_By_Neil /Where_do_you_get_your_ideas%3F.

4. Sarah Perez, "Report: Voice Assistants in Use to Triple to 8 Billion by 2023," *Tech Crunch*, February 12, 2019, https://techcrunch.com/2019/02/12 /report-voice-assistants-in-use-to-triple-to-8-billion-by-2023/.

5. Canadian Down Syndrome Society and Google AI, "Teaching Google to Understand People with Down Syndrome, One Voice at a Time," Project Understood, accessed May 16, 2022, https://projectunderstood.ca/.

6. "FCB Canada Is Teaching Google to Understand People with Down Syndrome," Little Black Book, November 5, 2019, https://www.lbbonline .com/news/fcb-canada-is-teaching-google-to-understand-people-with-down -syndrome.

7. Canadian Down Syndrome Society and Google AI, "Teaching Google to Understand People."

8. "FCB Canada Is Teaching Google to Understand People with Down Syndrome," Little Black Book.

9. "Canadian Down Syndrome Society and FCB Canada Launch 'Project Understood,'" Interpublic, November 22, 2019, https://www.interpublic.com /case-study/canadian-down-syndrome-society-and-fcb-canada-launch-project -understood/.

10. Megan Garber, "Instagram Was First Called 'Burbn,'" *The Atlantic*, July 2, 2014, https://www.theatlantic.com/technology/archive/2014/07/instagram -used-to-be-called-brbn/373815/.

11. "Glaucoma Sensor Team Wins National Dyson Design Award," National University of Singapore, news release, November 17, 2021, https://cde.nus.edu.sg /mse/news/glaucoma-sensor-team-wins-national-dyson-design-award/.

12. "International Winner: HOPES," James Dyson Award, accessed May 16, 2022, https://www.jamesdysonaward.org/en-US/2021/project/hopes/.

13. "What Is the History of Khan Academy?" Khan Academy, accessed May

16, 2022, https://support.khanacademy.org/hc/en-us/articles/202483180-What
-is-the-history-of-Khan-Academy-.

Chapter 4. Gap

1. Elijah Chiland, "Technology Week: Inversion Space Sets Sights on Returnable Rockets with Seed Funding," *Los Angeles Business Journal*, November 29, 2021, https://labusinessjournal.com/technology/inversion-space-sets-sights -returnable-rockets-see/.

2. Dennis Overbye, "Webb Telescope Prepares to Ascend, with an Eye toward Our Origins," *New York Times*, December 20, 2021, https://www.nytimes .com/2021/12/20/science/webb-telescope-astronomy.html?referringSource= articleShare.

3. Overbye, "Webb Telescope Prepares to Ascend."

4. "The LEGO Group Reveals First Prototype LEGO® Brick Made from Recycled Plastic," LEGO, June 22, 2021, https://www.lego.com/en-us/aboutus /news/2021/june/prototype-lego-brick-recycled-plastic/.

5. The Uncensored Library, accessed May 16, 2022, https://www.uncensored library.com/en.

6. Nik Popli, "The Best Inventions of 2021: A Compassionate Robot," *Time*, November 10, 2021, https://time.com/collection/best-inventions-2021/6113107 /robin-the-robot/.

7. "Robin the Robot: Meet Robin," Expper Technologies, accessed May 16, 2022, https://www.expper.tech/.

8. Melanie A. Farmer, "Lights! Camera! Algorithms?" *Columbia Magazine*, Spring 2017, https://magazine.columbia.edu/article/lights-camera-algorithms #:~:text=%E2%80%9COur%20insights%20are%20applicable%20to,program %20computers%20at%20age%20nine.

9. Maura Judkis, "Ramen, Noise, and Rebellion," *Washington Post*, September 19, 2019, https://www.washingtonpost.com/graphics/2019/lifestyle/food/david -chang/.

10. Kat Eschner, "Why the Can Opener Wasn't Invented until Almost 50 Years after the Can," *Smithsonian Magazine*, August 24, 2017, https://www .smithsonianmag.com/smart-news/why-can-opener-wasnt-invented-until-almost -50-years-after-can-180964590/.

11. The Write Channel with Nicola Monaghan, "Famous Writers Talk Ideas! Stephen King, John Irving, and Alan Hollinghurst Reveal Their Secrets," YouTube, January 29, 2017, https://www.youtube.com/watch?v=SKn3_BSQojo; Lane Florsheim, "My Monday Morning: Stephen King's Daily Routine Involves Four Hours of Writing and a Nap in the Afternoon," *Wall Street Journal*, June 7, 2021, https://www.wsj.com/articles/stephen-kings-daily-routine-involves-four -hours-of-writing-and-a-nap-in-the-afternoon-11623068593.

12. John Irving, "Last Night in Twisted River," John Irving, accessed May 26, 2022, https://john-irving.com/last-night-in-twisted-river-introduced-by-john-irving/.

13. The Write Channel with Nicola Monaghan, "Famous Writers Talk Ideas!"

14. Alexis Kriegh, "Café de la Rotonde," W&L Paris, accessed May 16, 2022, https://omeka.wlu.edu/wluparis/items/show/8.

15. Benedict Carey, "You're Bored, but Your Brain Is Tuned In," *New York Times*, August 5, 2008, https://www.nytimes.com/2008/08/05/health/research/05mind.html.

16. Caroline Newman, "What Actually Happens When Your Mind Wanders? This Professor Can Tell You," *Inside Higher Education*, accessed May 14, 2022, https://sponsored.chronicle.com/what-actually-happens-when-your-mind-wanders/index.html.

17. Newman, "What Actually Happens."

Chapter 5. Gain

1. "About Us," KlickEngage, accessed May 16, 2022, https://www.klickengage.com/about-us.

2. "How It Works," KlickEngage, accessed May 16, 2022, https://www.klickengage.com/how-klickengage-works.

3. "About Us," KlickEngage.

4. "International Top 20: Quito," James Dyson Award, accessed May 16, 2022, https://www.jamesdysonaward.org/en-AU/2020/project/quito/.

5. John Wray, "Haruki Murakami: The Art of Fiction No. 182," *Paris Review*, issue 170 (Summer 2004), https://www.theparisreview.org/interviews/2/the-art-of-fiction-no-182-haruki-murakami.

6. "Mission," Kuleana, accessed May 16, 2022, https://www.kuleana.co/mission.

7. "Case Database: Household Supplies & Services: United States: 2020 Silver Lysol," Effie, accessed May 16, 2022, https://www.effie.org/case_database/case/US_2020_E-5227-834.

8. Michael Paulson, "'Slave Play' Was Shut Out at the Tonys. But It's Coming Back to Broadway," *New York Times*, September 27, 2021, https://www.nytimes.com/2021/09/27/theater/slave-play-returning-broadway.html.

9. Tonya Pinkins, "'Slave Play': Racism Doesn't Have a Safe Word," *American Theatre*, July 1, 2019, https://www.americantheatre.org/2019/07/01/slave-play-racism-doesnt-have-a-safe-word/.

10. Ari Shapiro, "With 'Slave Play,' a Young Playwright Provokes His Way to Broadway," NPR, September 20, 2019, https://www.npr.org/2019/09/20/762785319/with-slave-play-a-youngplaywright-provokes-his-way-to-broadway.

Chapter 6. Diversity, Equity, and Inclusion

1. Ros Atkins, "The 50:50 Story," BBC, accessed May 16, 2022, https://www.bbc.co.uk/5050/aboutus/ourstory/.

2. Atkins, "The 50:50 Story."

3. Aneeta Rattan, Siri Chilazi, Oriane Georgeac, and Iris Bohnet, "Tackling the Underrepresentation of Women in Media," *Harvard Business Review,* June 6, 2019, https://hbr.org/2019/06/tackling-the-underrepresentation-of-women-in-media.

4. Nina Goswami, "The 50:50 Story," BBC, accessed June 26, 2022, https://www.bbc.co.uk/5050/aboutus/ourstory/.

5. "Case Study: Luis von Ahn," History Associates Incorporated, February 10, 2021, https://lemelson.mit.edu/sites/default/files/2021-02/LMIT_vonAhn_CaseStudy_0.pdf.

6. "Case Study: Luis von Ahn," History Associates Incorporated.

7. "Case Study: Luis von Ahn," History Associates Incorporated.

8. "Case Study: Luis von Ahn," History Associates Incorporated.

9. Jayme Fraser, "New Federal Requirements Show Airlines Damage Thousands of Wheelchairs Each Year," *USA Today,* November 22, 2019, https://www.usatoday.com/story/news/nation/2019/11/22/airlines-department-transportation-report-damagewheelchairs/4270695002/.

10. Fraser, "New Federal Requirements."

11. "Revolve Air Foldable Promises to Revolutionize Travel for Active Wheelchair Users," *Newz Hook,* March 17, 2021, http://newzhook.com/story/air-andrea-mocellin-disabled-revolve-air-foldable-wheelchair-wheelchair-accessibility/.

12. "Revolve Air Foldable," *Newz Hook.*

13. L. Tan, X. Wang, C. Guo, R. Zeng, T. Zhou, and G. Cao, "Does Exposure to Foreign Culture Influence Creativity? Maybe It's Not Only Due to Concept Expansion," *Frontiers in Psychology* 10 (April 11, 2019): 537, https://www.frontiersin.org/articles/10.3389/fpsyg.2019.00537/full.

14. J. G. Lu, A. C. Hafenbrack, P. W. Eastwick, D. J. Wang, W. W. Maddux, and A. D. Galinsky, "'Going Out' of the Box: Close Intercultural Friendships and Romantic Relationships Spark Creativity, Workplace Innovation, and Entrepreneurship," *Journal of Applied Psychology* 102, no. 7 (2017): 1091–1108, https://doi.org/10.1037/apl0000212.

15. Frédéric C. Godart, William W. Maddux, Andrew V. Shipilov, and Adam D. Galinsky, "Fashion with a Foreign Flair: Professional Experiences Abroad Facilitate the Creative Innovations of Organizations," *Academy of Management Journal* 58, no. 1 (February 2015): 195–220, https://journals.aom.org/doi/abs/10.5465/amj.2012.0575.

16. "About Us," Silkroad, accessed May 16, 2022, https://www.silkroad.org /about.

17. Tom Huizenga, "Can Yo-Yo Ma Fix the Arts?" NPR, April 9, 2013, https:// www.npr.org/sections/deceptivecadence/2013/04/09/176681242/can-yo-yo -ma-fix-the-arts.

18. Huizenga, "Can Yo-Yo Ma Fix the Arts?"

19. Katherine W. Phillips, "How Diversity Makes Us Smarter," *Greater Good Magazine*, September 18, 2017, https://greatergood.berkeley.edu/article/item /how_diversity_makes_us_smarter.

20. Inga J. Hoever, Daan Van Knippenberg, Wendy P. van Ginkel, and Harry G. Barkema, "Fostering Team Creativity: Perspective Taking as Key to Unlocking Diversity's Potential," *Journal of Applied Psychology* 97, no. 5 (2012): 982–96, https://pubmed.ncbi.nlm.nih.gov/22774764/.

21. Sundiatu Dixon-Fyle, Kevin Dolan, Vivian Hunt, and Sara Prince, "Diversity Wins: How Inclusion Matters," McKinsey & Company, May 19, 2020, https://www.mckinsey.com/featured-insights/diversity-and-inclusion/diversity -wins-how-inclusion-matters.

22. Dixon-Fyle et al., "Diversity Wins."

23. Manasi Sakpal, "Diversity and Inclusion Build High-Performance Teams," Gartner, September 20, 2019, https://www.gartner.com/smarterwithgartner /diversity-and-inclusion-build-high-performance-teams.

24. Robin J. Ely and David A. Thomas, "Getting Serious about Diversity: Enough Already with the Business Case," *Harvard Business Review*, November– December 2020, https://hbr.org/2020/11/getting-serious-about-diversity -enough-already-with-the-business-case.

25. Robin Landa, "Interview with Dr. Donald R. Marks," *Strategic Creativity* (New York: Routledge, 2022).

26. Robin Landa, "Interview with Rich Tu," *Strategic Creativity* (New York: Routledge, 2022).

27. Hanna Rantala, "Afghan Refugee Shares Secret Story in Acclaimed Film 'Flee,'" Reuters, February 7, 2022, https://www.reuters.com/article/film-flee -idCAKBN2KC1OR.

28. Lisa Abend, "A Refugee's Harrowing Story, Finally Told through Animation," *New York Times*, November 26, 2021, https://www.nytimes.com/2021 /11/26/movies/flee-movie-jonas-poher-rasmussen.html.

29. Abend, "A Refugee's Harrowing Story."

30. David Gianatasio, "Droga5 Fights Anti-AAPI Bigotry with 'I'm Really From' Travel Posters," *Muse by Clio*, November 19, 2021, https://musebycl.io/art /droga5-fights-anti-aapi-bigotry-really-travel-posters.

31. Andrew Limbong, "Microaggressions Are a Big Deal: How to Talk Them Out and When to Walk Away," NPR, June 9, 2020, https://www.npr.org/2020/06

/08/872371063/microaggressions-are-a-big-deal-how-to-talk-them-out-and-when
-to-walk-away.

32. "Seeing Something in a New Way Is Seeing It for the First Time," B2 F4
flyer, 1980, Richard Wilde Papers, School of Visual Arts Archives, New York,
https://archives.sva.edu/collection-guide/richard-wilde-papers.

Chapter 7. Emotional Obstacles

1. Dan Pashman, "Mission ImPASTAble," *Sporkful,* November 8, 2021, https://
www.sporkful.com/tag/mission-impastable/.

2. Dom Nero, "He Spent Three Years Inventing a Pasta Shape. It Puts
Spaghetti to Shame," *Esquire,* March 31, 2021, https://www.esquire.com/food
-drink/food/a35983074/new-pasta-shape-invented-dan-pashman-interview/.

3. Ashlie D. Stevens, "Everything You Need to Know about Cascatelli, the
New 'Perfect' Pasta Shape That's a Viral Hit," *Salon,* March 29, 2021, https://
www.salon.com/2021/03/29/what-to-know-about-cascatelli-pasta/.

4. Stuart Jeffries, "Squid Games Creator: I'm Not That Rich. It's Not Like
Netflix Paid Me a Bonus," *Guardian,* October 26, 2021, https://www.theguardian
.com/tv-and-radio/2021/oct/26/squid-games-creator-rich-netflix-bonus-hwang
-dong-hyuk.

5. Jeffries, "Squid Games Creator."

6. "The Making of a Global Sensation: The Journey to Creating Squid
Games," Netflix, September 29, 2021, https://about.netflix.com/en/news/the
-making-of-a-global-sensation-the-journey-to-creating-squid-game.

Conclusion

1. Twyla Tharp, *The Creative Habit: Learn It and Use It for Life* (New York:
Simon and Schuster, 2006), 12.

2. United Nations, "The 17 Goals," accessed May 16, 2022, https://sdgs.un
.org/goals.

Resource 3. How Diversity, Equity, and Inclusion Can Amplify the Three Gs

1. "Comparison of Dialogue and Debate," United States Institute of Peace
Global Campus, 2015, https://www.usip.org/sites/default/files/2017-01/Dialog
ue%2Bvs%2BDebate%2B-%2BUSIP%2BGlobal%2BCampus.pdf.

ACKNOWLEDGMENTS

Not since graduate school have I met someone who has taught me as much as Steve Piersanti, founder and senior editor of Berrett-Koehler. Steve Piersanti has been my Batman, my guru, and the wisest and most supportive editor any author could desire. This book would not be the same without him. There are only a few people who have changed my life and work for the better— Steve is one of them. I owe him a deep debt of gratitude.

When I first witnessed Holly Taylor's talent, it was on my television screen when she was playing Paige Jennings in *The Americans*. Then I had the opportunity to witness her vast talent in person at Kean University, when she was my student and created an outstanding portfolio of creative design and advertising. Now we have collaborated to bring this book to life. Thank you, Holly, for sharing this creative journey with me.

When I first saw Lorin Latarro, she was performing on Broadway. Later I was fortunate to get to know her as a brilliant Broadway director and choreographer. My great thanks to Lorin. As I said to her when I read her foreword, "Is there anything you can't do?"

The folks at Berrett-Koehler were a delight to work with—not only my exceptional editor, Steve, but also all the wonderful people who supported this book from start to finish: María Jesús Aguiló, Charlotte Ashlock, Tryn Brown, Valerie Caldwell, Leslie Crandell, Michael Crowley, Dr. Tricia Farwell, Maren Fox, Kristen Frantz, Kylie Johnston, Shanzeh Khurram, Catherine Lengronne,

David Marshall, Sarah Modlin, Courtney Schonfeld, Katie Sheehan, Jeevan Sivasubramaniam, Johanna Vondeling, Edward Wade, and other BK staff whom I haven't named. Great thanks to peer reviewers Nic Albert, Rachel Henry, and Chloe Lizotte, who offered terrific advice. My thanks to Janet Reed Blake, Dave Peattie of BookMatters, and Leonard Rosenbaum for their support. Special thanks to copy editor Heidi Fritschel.

To Kean University's president, Dr. Lamont Repollet, and provost and senior vice president, Dr. David Birdsell, I owe immense debts of gratitude. At Kean University, I gratefully acknowledge Dr. Joy Moskovitz, assistant provost and vice president; David Mohney, dean of the Michael Graves College; Rose Gonnella, associate dean of the Michael Graves College; Reenat Hasan Munshi, managing director of the Office of Release Time and Sponsored Programs, and the Release Time for Research Committee; Professor Denise Anderson, Professor Ed Johnston, Professor Craig Konyk, Professor Linda O'Shea, and all my colleagues in the Michael Graves College.

Professional creatives, colleagues, and students took the time to read my manuscript, contribute their expertise, support my project, or offer feedback about the Three Gs. I am grateful to David Baldwin, Arnold Calderon, Jessica Castillo, Bernice Chao, Dr. Jennifer Chen, Ross Chowles, Randy Clark, Dayle of Artful City Style, Dusty Crocker, Nicholas D'Angelo, Kayla Darcy, Meaghan Dee, Dr. Tricia M. Farwell, Sarah Goforth, Pancho González, David Gottwald, Dr. Todd Greer, Stacey Hall, Leslie Haines, Jessica Hawkins, Rob Jolles, Dominic Katransky, Dr. Donald R. Marks, Shannon McCarthy, Dawnmarie McDermid, Ana Carolina Mitchell, Christopher Navetta, Dr. Bob Nelson, Elena Pejovska, Alison Place, Romit Sarkar, Debra Satterfield, Mike Schnaidt, Aaris Sherin, Camille Sherrod, Michael Sherrod, Patrycja Sliwowska, Aggie Toppins,

Rich Tu, Dr. Gregory Turner-Rahman, Natalie Tyree, Lillianna Vazquez, Alejandra Vidal, and Donna Wertalik.

I hope I haven't forgotten anyone.

Loving thanks to Deborah Ceballos; Rose Gonnella; my husband, Dr. Harry Gruenspan; and our daughter, Hayley, who tenderly supported me during this project (and pretty much through everything).

NOTES: YOUR IDEAS

What's your goal?

_____

_____

_____

What gap does your goal fill?

_____

_____

_____

Who will gain?

_____

_____

_____

Your Worthwhile Idea:

_____

_____

_____

INDEX

ABOUT THE AUTHOR

When Robin's student Brooke returned from her first week as an intern at a top New York City advertising agency, she said, "I was the only one on my team who rattled off one good idea after another. My creative director said we could use all my ideas. The other interns just sat there."

Now Brooke is a senior art director at another top New York ad agency, where she creates award-winning ad campaigns for national brands. So are thousands of Robin's other former students, who are award-winning professionals working in advertising and design, creativity-dependent businesses demanding many ideas daily.

Called "one of the great teachers of our time" by the Carnegie Foundation, Robin holds the title of Distinguished Professor in the Michael Graves College of Kean University. She has taught university students as well as trained industry professionals to generate lots of worthwhile ideas. It's no surprise people consider Robin a creativity guru. But she's more than that—Robin uses her creative powers for good.

With a strong moral compass, she asks her university students, the faculty she mentors, as well as the many Fortune 500 clients she advises, "How does your goal benefit individuals, society, or our planet? How can your idea make life better?" Robin champions her university students; advocates for industry diversity, equity, and inclusion; and provides university scholarships for meritorious students as well as students in need.

Like many creatives, Robin produces ideas in various forms—writing, design, advertising, fine art, screenwriting, and of course, her pedagogy. All of these endeavors feed her creative thinking and ability to communicate how to be strategically creative to others. She is the author of twenty-five books, including *Strategic Creativity: A Business Field Guide for Advertising, Branding and Design; Graphic Design Solutions* (sixth edition); *Advertising by Design* (fourth edition); and *Nimble: Thinking Creatively in the Digital Age.* Through her published tomes, Robin's ideas teach people worldwide.

Robin has been recognized many times for her design, writing, teaching, art, and research, with awards from, among others, the National Society of Arts and Letters, the Art Directors Club of New Jersey, Graphic Design USA, and the National League of American Pen Women. She was named Kean University 2013 Teacher of the Year and received several Kean Presidential Excellence awards for research. For her humanitarian work, she received the 2015 Human Rights Educator award, and her student design team won humanitarian awards as well.

For six years, Robin was a cochair of Design Incubation, a national design research organization, and she has juried design and advertising competitions. *Crack the Spine* literary journal published several short stories by Robin, and the journal's editor nominated Robin's story "Just Desserts" for Best of the Net. Recently, Robin presented about personal branding at Columbia University. She is currently co-writing a book with Greg Braun, retired deputy global chief creative officer of Commonwealth/McCann, titled *Sharewor-thy: Storytelling for Advertising* for Columbia University Press.

When she's not writing, teaching, or consulting, you can find Robin dancing with her husband or watching *Jeopardy* with their daughter in her hometown of New York City.

About the Illustrator/Designer

Holly Taylor's first words were, "I'm going to be on Broadway." OK. Maybe not her *first* words, but that's a pretty bold statement for a three-year-old. Bold statements like that have been mani-festing themselves in unexpected ways throughout Holly's life. One of them— "I'd love to illustrate a book one day"—is manifesting itself right here in *The New Art of Ideas: Unlock Your Creative Potential.*

A curious creative since childhood, Holly began her career at age eleven in *Billy Elliot* on Broadway, where she played Sharon Percy, a big-headed ballerina on pointe. After two years of perfor-mances, Holly was relieved to realize that acting meant playing a different person and that no one in the audience actually thought Holly was big-headed herself, so she decided to give acting a real try in Los Angeles. She ended up playing Paige Jennings on FX's critically acclaimed drama series *The Americans* for six years. From there she has stepped into the shoes of other characters in projects like *The Good Doctor, The Unsettling,* and *Dolly Parton's Heartstrings.* Most recently, she has played Angelina Meyer on *Manifest.* She is extra thankful that people can separate the character from the actor in this case (meaning: the character is a nut job).

Throughout this ever-changing and unpredictable journey through the performing arts, there has been one constant: Holly's desire to be educated. She attended public middle school and high school in New Jersey while working, maintaining her honor roll standing, and participating in multiple student organizations. Seeking a backup plan in case the whole acting thing didn't work out, Holly decided a degree in advertising design would be a smart balance between creativity and corporate opportunity. The Michael Graves College at Kean University provided an opportunity for higher education that could coexist with her acting schedule. While studying advertising design, Holly was advised and taught by the inspiring Robin Landa. Robin's dedication to students, ever-growing curiosity, unique artistic talents, and passion for building a better future made her an inspiration to Holly and all students at Kean. Without her guidance or trust, Holly would not have been able to pursue her passion for design, fine arts, or creative thinking in such a nourishing environment.

Holly now lives in New York City, where she shoots *Manifest* while doing freelance design work for nonprofits, start-ups, friends, and her own sanity. You can find Holly Taylor on Netflix or at https:// hollytaylor.design/.

Berrett–Koehler
Publishers

Berrett-Koehler is an independent publisher dedicated to an ambitious mission: *Connecting people and ideas to create a world that works for all.*

Our publications span many formats, including print, digital, audio, and video. We also offer online resources, training, and gatherings. And we will continue expanding our products and services to advance our mission.

We believe that the solutions to the world's problems will come from all of us, working at all levels: in our society, in our organizations, and in our own lives. Our publications and resources offer pathways to creating a more just, equitable, and sustainable society. They help people make their organizations more humane, democratic, diverse, and effective (and we don't think there's any contradiction there). And they guide people in creating positive change in their own lives and aligning their personal practices with their aspirations for a better world.

And we strive to practice what we preach through what we call "The BK Way." At the core of this approach is *stewardship,* a deep sense of responsibility to administer the company for the benefit of all of our stakeholder groups, including authors, customers, employees, investors, service providers, sales partners, and the communities and environment around us. Everything we do is built around stewardship and our other core values of *quality, partnership, inclusion,* and *sustainability.*

This is why Berrett-Koehler is the first book publishing company to be both a B Corporation (a rigorous certification) and a benefit corporation (a for-profit legal status), which together require us to adhere to the highest standards for corporate, social, and environmental performance. And it is why we have instituted many pioneering practices (which you can learn about at www.bkconnection.com), including the Berrett-Koehler Constitution, the Bill of Rights and Responsibilities for BK Authors, and our unique Author Days.

We are grateful to our readers, authors, and other friends who are supporting our mission. We ask you to share with us examples of how BK publications and resources are making a difference in your lives, organizations, and communities at www.bkconnection.com/impact.

Dear reader,

Thank you for picking up this book and welcome to the worldwide BK community! You're joining a special group of people who have come together to create positive change in their lives, organizations, and communities.

What's BK all about?

Our mission is to connect people and ideas to create a world that works for all.

Why? Our communities, organizations, and lives get bogged down by old paradigms of self-interest, exclusion, hierarchy, and privilege. But we believe that can change. That's why we seek the leading experts on these challenges—and share their actionable ideas with you.

A welcome gift

To help you get started, we'd like to offer you a **free copy** of one of our bestselling ebooks:

www.bkconnection.com/welcome

When you claim your **free ebook**, you'll also be subscribed to our blog.

Our freshest insights

Access the best new tools and ideas for leaders at all levels on our blog at ideas.bkconnection.com.

Sincerely,

Your friends at Berrett-Koehler

Certified

Corporation